GREAT INNOVATION IDEAS

Howard Wright

Marshall Cavendish
Business

Published in 2012 by Marshall Cavendish Business
An imprint of Marshall Cavendish International

PO Box 65829
London EC1P 1NY, United Kingdom
info@marshallcavendish.co.uk
and
1 New Industrial Road, Singapore 536196
genrefsales@sg.marshallcavendish.com
www.marshallcavendish.com/genref

Other Marshall Cavendish offices: Marshall Cavendish International (Asia) Private Limited, 1 New Industrial Road, Singapore 536196 • Marshall Cavendish Corporation. 99 White Plains Road, Tarrytown NY 10591-9001, USA • Marshall Cavendish International (Thailand) Co Ltd. 253 Asoke, 12th Flr, Sukhumvit 21 Road, Klongtoey Nua, Wattana, Bangkok 10110, Thailand • Marshall Cavendish (Malaysia) Sdn Bhd, Times Subang, Lot 46, Subang Hi-Tech Industrial Park, Batu Tiga, 40000 Shah Alam, Selangor Darul Ehsan, Malaysia

Marshall Cavendish is a trademark of Times Publishing Limited

A CIP record for this book is available from the British Library

ISBN 978-981-4351-22-5

Printed and bound in by CPI Group (UK) Ltd, Croydon, CR0 4YY

CONTENTS

Part 3 – People

Part 4 – Process

Part 5 – Research

Part 6 – Technique

Appendix

This book is dedicated to my wife, Lorna, for her encouragement
and patience in helping me complete it.

I would also like to thank Maureen Gardiner for her
inspiration and support.

INTRODUCTION

What is innovation?

"There's a way to do it better, find it."

Thomas Edison

THERE ARE MANY different theories that explain what innovation really is: radical, breakthrough, disruptive, incremental, open, hybrid are just a few that are discussed in the numerous books, websites and academic journals available today. There are arguments stating that an innovation has to have a disruptive effect to qualify as innovative; others argue that any change, as long as it is measurable, can be considered an innovation.

These different interpretations of innovation are typically based on perception as there is no definitive definition of the word which has become synonymous with 'new' and 'change', although it can just as easily be applied to incremental and evolution. It is an inspirational word with many connotations and associations, and companies around the world include it in their marketing materials as well as in their reports and accounts. How individuals and companies define innovation can have a dramatic affect on how they measure success.

When every new product or service claims to be 'innovative', it becomes difficult to say what innovation really is. Simply stating that a new product/service/business model is innovative without a definitive definition makes it difficult to assess whether the assertion is true or merely a rehash of the old.

A quick search on Amazon (UK) brings up over 45,000 titles in hardcover, and more than 112,000 titles overall, that contain the word innovation. A Google search reveals 70 million websites that refer to the 'definition of innovation'. Clearly, everyone seems to be talking about it but there seems to be a high degree of ambiguity and misunderstanding about the topic.

To try to make things a little clearer, I have put together six approaches that seem to be in common usage around the world.

1. Innovation is invention

"Creativity is thinking up new things. Innovation is doing new things."
Theodore Levitt

For many, innovation is about invention and this is reflected in the Oxford English Dictionary's definition:

> *The introduction of novelties; the alteration of what is established by the introduction of new elements or forms. A change made in the nature or fashion of anything; something newly introduced; a novel practice, method, etc. The action of introducing a new product into the market; a product newly brought on to the market.*

Although invention is clearly an element of innovation, it is only a part of it and the real benefits from innovation activities come from implementation – making something real and deriving some form of value from the idea.

There is however, some confusion about the difference between innovation and creativity. Are they the same or fundamentally different? I like to use the Attitude Skill and Knowledge (ASK) Diagram, which attempts to identify the dimensions of these two areas.

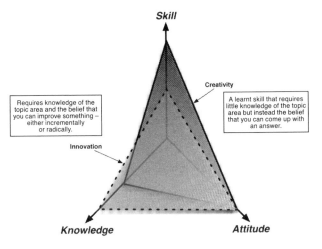

Figure 1: ASK Diagram

The diagram shows that to be creative you do not need a huge amount of knowledge, just the skill to understand and apply the various techniques, and an attitude that allows you to do so. Anyone can come up with a new design for a car or a stamp, but without applying it, it would be just an idea.

Alternatively, it can be argued that innovativeness requires some knowledge about the industry, as it is the different applications of this knowledge that can make the breakthrough innovative.

To me, innovation is not a skill; it cannot be taught the way creativity techniques can. Instead it is more a state of mind, an attitude that 'allows' people to use the knowledge and experience they have in new ways. The ability to find new ways of doing things is present in all of us, but it is the confidence to do something about it that sets true innovators apart from the rest.

2. Innovation is incremental change

"Future economic prosperity depends on building a new, stronger foundation and recapturing the 'spirit of innovation'."

President Obama (January 2011)

It is sometimes argued that innovation is not radical but instead denotes 'incremental improvements' that can be capitalised on and turned into significant change for the organisation – a bottom up approach. An example of this is Apple Inc. – instead of inventing new things, Apple took a completely different view towards what was already there. For instance, it took the MP3 player and used its flair for design to create the iPod; similarly the iPad built on the existing tablet computers.

3. Innovation is the 'silver bullet' – the answer

Innovation is one of those activities that seems to go in and out of fashion, with companies investing and de-investing on a regular basis. When in 'vogue' everything and everyone claims to be innovative.

Although this can initially affect the organisation and those involved, this approach is typically short-lived as a realisation that commitment is waning takes hold. In recent times, it is efficiency initiatives such as Six Sigma and Lean Manufacturing that many organisations are involved in, but it is debatable whether these can be termed truly innovative.

Organisations that have a tendency to follow this trend keep finding new 'silver bullets' to solve their problems. Unfortunately the reality is that none of them do, and this indicates a more fundamental, underlying problem within the company.

4. Innovation is marketing hype

With everyone claiming to have products and services that are innovative, the term loses value and becomes meaningless. If you do a quick search on the report and accounts of the FTSE 100 companies in the UK, you will find most firms claiming to be innovative, or undertaking innovation activities. This may be true, but it is more likely to be marketing hype. In this definition, innovation activity has little or no real value.

5. Innovation is about subversive change

Many individuals who have a stake in maintaining the status quo within an organisation or are involved in long-term strategy hold this view. My mantra when running an innovation team was 'ask for forgiveness not for permission' and this approach has worked for me for the over 15 years I have worked in the innovation field (I was called in to my boss twice to apologise). What I did come to realise is that subversive change can be bad as it excludes people from the process and therefore holds back acceptance and ownership.

6. Innovation is about improvement

One of my favourite definitions of innovation comes from David Neeleman, founder of JetBlue: "Innovation is trying to figure out a way to do something better than it's ever been done before." To me this encapsulates the true essence of innovation – yes there is an element of invention, but it is also about implementing these ideas or solutions and creating value for the individual or the company.

100 Great Innovation Ideas is based on my own experience of working in innovation since 1994. The innovation journey has been a rollercoaster – I have had periods of tremendous elation and troughs of despair, and real successes that added huge amounts of value to the company as well as unexpected outcomes (I don't call them failures), which have been disappointing. Through all this I have learnt much about the 'beast' that is innovation and have tapped into this experience to share some useful pointers, tools and techniques in this book.

There is no magic formula when it comes to innovation. There is no single textbook you can refer to, or framework that will solve all your problems. Innovation is about what is right for you at a particular time and in a particular situation.

By buying this book you have taken the first step to becoming a true innovator, you have shown that you have the curiosity and the desire to do things differently. The next step is a change in attitude; grow the confidence to do things differently. Start small and reward yourself along the way. Look for interesting problems to tackle, find new areas of interest that will foster new insights and provide a nursery for new ideas.

This book provides you with 100 ideas to use when approaching innovation, either as an individual, as a consultant or as an employee of a company. It is not intended that the reader start at the beginning and read through to the end, but rather dip in and out as and when required.

The secret to successful innovation is to remain curious, stay positive, retain your enthusiasm and, above all, believe in yourself, and keep moving forward!

PART 1
APPROACH

Your attitude and approach to innovation is one of the key success factors. Often the only thing that separates great innovators from the rest of society is their attitude, their curiosity and can-do mentality.

TAKE A BREAK FROM TECHNOLOGY

"In your success... it's not a matter of being in the right place at the right time nearly as much as it is a matter of taking the time to determine what the right place and time ought to be!"

Denis Waitley

The idea

The day-to-day pressures of life mean that we often do not have time to ponder new ideas. Since the invention of the Gutenberg Printing Press, we have been producing more books and information than an average human being could ever read in their lifetime. The beauty, and irony, of Gutenberg's invention was the ability to produce a mass amount of books at an extremely low cost. This resulted in the unfamiliar dilemma of having a wide choice of books to read, and the beginning of what is now called information overload.

Today we have computers, iPhones, iPads, Kindles and Blackberries that feed us with gigabytes of information at even lower cost. We are bombarded with advertising, entertainment, news, music, text messages, phone calls... the list goes on.

Unfortunately, much of the information we receive is of little value. We are increasingly being driven by technology – we have to answer that text, constantly check our messages during dinner, even in the toilet; interestingly, in the UK, as many as 150,000 phones are dropped down the WC every year!

Facebook and Twitter are other sources of information overload. They can be useful tools for sharing information, but when taken to the extreme, they can become a colossal waste of time.

While the printing press helped make books easily available, the Internet has caused an exponential growth in information. In January 2011, there were over 275 million websites brimming over with facts, tips, news and general wisdom – double the number in 2008! The Internet has made massive amounts of information more accessible than anyone could have ever imagined or predicted.

With this information overload, how can we think?

To function effectively, the brain needs time and space to process the tsunami of stimulus it receives. The idea of 'going off grid' has become increasingly popular as people recognise the pressures that technology has brought into their lives.

The first step is to evaluate your day. How much time do you spend responding, interacting and reacting to technology – be it email, phone, TV or the microwave? You may be surprised at how much technology has come to rule your life. Ask yourself "what would I do if I didn't have any of these things?". It may be time to re-evaluate how you live, decide what is important to you and re-establish control over your life.

Giving yourself time and space to think is fundamental to becoming more innovative.

In practice

- Give yourself some time to think. Take an hour off and sit in a park and do nothing – you will be surprised at the ideas that come to you.

- Make sure the junk filter on your email account is switched on and optimised.

- Set aside a day a week to switch off all electronic communication. This will be hard at first but keep at it. Use the time to do something you enjoy.

- Employ an active communication management strategy to reduce the e-clutter in your life.

2 REWARD INNOVATION AND CREATIVITY

"Just as energy is the basis of life itself, and ideas the source of innovation, so is innovation the vital spark of all human change, improvement and progress."

Ted Levitt

The idea

There is a need to reinforce exceptional behaviour, and none more so than innovation and creativity. The rewards do not have to be big or even financial, but can be as small as a pat on the back, or appreciation for a job well done. Trying to tailor the reward to the individual can be rewarding in its own right.

Rewarding exceptional behaviour can be difficult at times as this kind of behaviour can sometimes prove to be disruptive, especially in large organisations. The use of non-financial rewards can in this situation be more appropriate, as it will be less visible and more personal.

Think back to when you were praised or rewarded, maybe when you were a child. How did you feel? Did it change you? Our childhood responses to praise and reward stay with us into adulthood, even though we tend to suppress them as we get older.

An important factor when thinking about rewards is not to overdo them. The overuse of a reward system can be as detrimental as underuse. Monitor their use and track the response – did it have the desired result? If not, try something different.

To encourage innovative behaviour, the following four elements can be valuable first steps to changing the culture of an organisation:

- Identify what people perceive as positive innovation.

- Ensure that performance management systems are clearly aligned with a culture of innovation.

- Ensure that the leadership and senior management demonstrate the desired behaviours.

- Create a 'safe' environment in which to put forward new ideas, make suggestions, question assumptions and challenge the status quo.

The important thing is to set goals and take action. Identify the behaviour you want to encourage and then do something about it. If we reward innovative behaviour we will get more such behaviour – if we ignore it we will lose it.

In practice

- Decide what the 'right' innovative behaviours are for you, document them and revisit them on a regular basis to see if they have changed. Do not be surprised if they have. Innovation is all about changing your behaviour and attitude. Update them as your views change or you get the opportunity to benchmark with other individuals or companies.

- Look for ways of rewarding incremental successes in small ways. Don't wait for the end of the project or the initiative; it may be too late to encourage the right attitude.

- Do not rely purely on cash rewards. Find new ways of rewarding innovative behaviour. Take the time to understand your team, your family or group. What reward would they most appreciate?

- Create a reward tracking system to monitor what works and what doesn't. If something doesn't work then don't use it again. Try something different and see what happens.

3 ACKNOWLEDGE AND CELEBRATE PROGRESS

"Short-term innovation alone will leave a company at a loss when the first competitor radically changes the game. Establishing permanent systemic creativity and instituting formal measures that encourage and capture rich and speculative thought from every creative problem-solving effort will boost a company's innovation potential well into the future."

Jeff Mauzy and Richard Harriman

The idea

Monitoring progress towards a goal is important when trying something new, and in fact, it can be more important to celebrate progress than it is to celebrate success.

Having a great idea or solution to a problem is just the starting point of any innovation activity – in reality a great idea has no real value unless something is done with it, and some value is created.

When I first started working in innovation in the mid 1990s, I thought innovation was just about having crazy ideas. I spent most of my time coming up with idea after idea but implementing nothing at all and feeling increasingly frustrated that my efforts were not being valued. It was not until someone asked me to produce a monthly progress update that I realised that what I was doing wasn't really innovation – it was just invention. I started tracking some of the ideas that groups had generated in workshops I was facilitating and found that those who were achieving success had developed tracking mechanisms, ways of monitoring the progress of an idea.

This realisation changed my behaviour, and instead of spending 90% of my time generating ideas, I began to spend 80% of my time monitoring implementation of the ideas I generated or facilitated. What resulted was not only a change in my, and my team's behaviour, but also a significant change in the perception of value the team generated, as well as a huge benefit to the company.

Although this example concerns innovation in a company, the lessons can be translated to home life too. If you have a great idea to redecorate a room or change the garden, setting out a plan and making a list of tasks, and then monitoring them, can keep you going when you feel like giving up. This way you can keep track of what you have achieved and how much you have to complete.

Nothing spurs you on more than identifying what you have achieved.

In practice

- Write down your idea or solution and make a list of the tasks you think you will need to do. Review your list weekly. Chart your progress and add any new tasks you have identified. This can be a simple Excel spreadsheet or if you have access to it, a project management package. Don't be put off by the technology though, the important thing is to record and track your progress.

- Chart your progress on your wall so you can see it every day – it will encourage you to keep going.

- Keep a success journal to record your successes and achievements. It is easy to forget what you have achieved at the end of the project; typically, we only remember the past few months and forget about things that have happened previously. By recording your achievements, you will be able to reflect on your progress and successes.

TAKE YOUR TIME

The idea

Our lives today are increasingly packed with activity we try to cram into our waking hours. We are driven by timescales and deadlines often imposed by other people, whether at home or at work. Technology has become an increasing pressure – we are always available, always reacting to emails, text messages and phone calls.

This frantic lifestyle leaves little time to think or to contemplate ideas and problems. We have become highly reactive, often choosing a 'firefighting' approach rather than more considered and thought-through action, choosing to fix things quickly and move on to the next thing. Even our holidays have become activity-based. We often choose to do and see numerous things, instead of relaxing and giving ourselves time to think.

In the many innovation models that have been developed, a key element is an incubation phase, the thinking time, which varies from 20% – 80% of the time allocated for an innovation initiative. Often this incubation period may occur before you have settled on the idea, when it may be measured in years rather than hours.

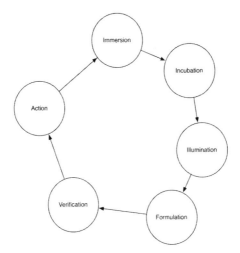

Figure 2: Creativity Cycle

Although many 'experts' place emphasis on information gathering, executing and measurement, they all agree that the 'process' of innovation requires time to consider the options, build linkages with other ideas and formulate the idea/solution. In the innovation model above, all but the action phase require time to think, contemplate, consider, generate ideas and verify.

Action is typically less than 20% of the total time of any innovation activity although it is 80% of the value. Incubation takes up 80% of the time.

In practice

- Write down your problem/opportunity/idea and then plan some 'downtime' each week. Try to spend at least two hours a week doing nothing but thinking about things. This doesn't have to be done all at once and can be broken down into smaller units, although I would recommend that each of these be at least 30 minutes long.

- Ensure you enjoy at least one vacation a year when you relax completely.

- Find your quiet special space where you can go to think.

BE PREPARED TO FAIL AND LEARN FROM IT

5

The idea

Many of us are brought up believing that failure is a bad thing; our early childhood experiences typically involve being admonished for getting things wrong. Although we have to learn the difference between right and wrong and what is 'good' and bad', we are often not taught how to learn from our mistakes.

The famous Thomas Edison story tells of how he invented the light bulb. He tried more than 2,000 experiments before he got the electric bulb to work. A reporter asked him how it felt to fail so many times, Edison responded, "I never failed once. I invented the light bulb. It just happened to be a 2,000 step process." At every stage, he learnt what worked and what did not. If he had given up at stage one, the world would be a darker place today!

The problem we have today is that we have a low tolerance for failure, particularly in a business environment. Failure or the perception of failure is often 'rewarded' with dismissal, although the reality is that although the expected results may not have been achieved, those involved learnt a valuable lesson.

Cause	%
Insufficient knowledge	36%
Underestimation of influence	18%
Ignorance, carelessness, negligence	14%
Forgetfulness, error	13%
Relying on others without sufficient control	9%
Unprecise definition of responsibilities	1%
Choice of poor quality materials	1%
Other	3%

Figure 3: Zurich Study of Major Engineering Failures

A 1976 study carried out by the Swiss Federal Institute of Technology in Zurich, on the reasons for major engineering failures, found insufficient knowledge to be their primary cause. The more information we have, the less likely we are to fail, so engineers today are more likely to get things right by learning from what didn't work in the past.

This is true for all aspects of our lives, whether it is work, at home or during leisure. We need to learn from our mistakes rather than trying to forget them and move on. In every situation, it can be worthwhile jotting down what has worked and what hasn't. Just the act of writing it down commits it to memory and can provide a useful reference when you face a similar situation or a new challenge.

Don't think about failure, instead think about unexpected outcomes!

In practice

- If something hasn't worked, don't focus on the failure, instead think about what did work and write it down.

- Think about what hasn't worked for you in the past and reflect on how you dealt with the situation and what you learnt. Was this a positive or negative experience? Did you come out of the situation a better person?

- Keep an outcome journal where you record things that worked, and what didn't work. Take time to reflect on these outcomes every month, noting what you learnt and what you would do differently in future.

TAKE CHANCES

"I believe that fate is choices, it's not chance."

Wayne Newton

The idea

Throughout our lives we are often warned against taking risks, which prevents us from taking even small chances. However, it is the chances that we take that can propel us the farthest. By taking chances we embrace new experiences and new opportunities.

In my career it has been the moments where I have taken a chance that have proved the most exciting, and interestingly, most profitable. Back in the 1980s, I was working for a large telecommunications company designing telecommunications networks for the financial services industry. One day I met a former manager in the lift and he asked if I would like to join a new computer group he was setting up; this was when computers were new and, for many, unknown. This was a risky step for me as it meant moving out of a safe and steady job into a team that didn't exist, working with people I had never met, and doing something I had little knowledge about. But I took the chance and what followed were ten of the most exciting years of my career.

I could have, like some of my colleagues, taken the safe route and stayed where I was. Instead, I decided to take a chance and it transformed my life.

Most of our experiences as children are about taking chances – if we aren't familiar with or don't know something, we still have a go at it.

We don't have the fear of being wrong, just the desire to find out. If you are not prepared to be wrong, you will never develop yourself or your idea. By the time we become adults, we have lost the capacity to take risks, and being wrong or being seen as wrong frightens us. Mistakes are perceived as a stigma, while successes are often ignored or forgotten about.

At a conference in 1991, Gerald Ratner, a successful jeweller in the UK, spoke about how bad his products were and subsequently, his business collapsed. This was ten years ago and yet it is still talked about, while nobody remembers the exceptional things he did before that speech.

We need to change from a system that punishes errors and drives them underground to one that celebrates an open approach – seeing problems not as faults to be punished but instead as important opportunities to improve both the product and ourselves.

The best risks to take are 'intelligent risks', where the potential downside is limited, but the potential upside is virtually unlimited. These are the risks you should jump to take.

In practice

- Do something you wouldn't normally do, something that is out of character or something that you have been scared of doing in the past. You'll soon realise that it was not that frightening after all.

- Think about a time when you took a risk. What was the outcome? Was it positive or negative?

- Read books about people who have taken risks; this can be a great way to inspire a change of attitude.

7 MAKE A MOVIE OF THE PROBLEM OR SITUATION

"At Wal-Mart, if you couldn't explain an idea in simple terms on one page of paper, Sam Walton considered the new idea too complicated to implement."

Michael Bergdahl

The idea

Translating your insight and vision into something everyone can understand can be a challenge. Your ability to see the problem or opportunity from a particular perspective is yours and yours alone. We often assume that everyone sees the world as we do, or has had the same experiences that we have had. The reality is that we are all unique.

What brought this to light for me was an innocent remark made by a friend while we were holidaying together in the US. One morning, as we walked into the restaurant of the hotel where we were staying, for breakfast, my friend asked me to pass him the yellow paper from the pile of newspapers lying on a table by the entrance. "Yellow?" I asked, "There is no yellow paper." To which he replied, "The yellow *Financial Times*." To me this paper looked pink, and to him it was yellow. He assumed that everyone saw the world as he did and I assumed the same. But in truth we all see the world differently.

Creating a visual representation of a problem or an opportunity can be highly beneficial. Making a movie of how things are now and how they could be, or how you envision them to be, can bring new insights as well as an important shared understanding. In this way, everyone sees the same thing and they all have the same understanding of it.

Video capture technology is available on most phones and cameras today and there are also a number of low-cost video cameras in the market.

But don't spend too much time on this – the more 'real' it is the better. Focus on capturing the salient points, perhaps from a specific individual's point of view.

By viewing the situation from the 'outside', you too can gain ideas and thoughts on how to make things happen, and even new insights into improving your idea.

In practice

- Try writing a story about your idea – make it a fairytale or a soap opera. Make a short movie with your colleagues, family members or a friend that describes the problem and your solution.

- Make a TV advertisement for your idea. Which 'famous person' would you have presenting it and what would the key message be?

- Write a conversation between two people in a cafe discussing the problem and your idea. Role-play and video it and watch it again to see if you gain any new insights.

- Consider making a 'day-in-the-life-of' documentary about someone, using your idea or solution.

BE OPEN TO NEW IDEAS

"When all think alike, then no one is thinking."

Walter Lippman

The idea

Innovation requires that we remain open to ideas that are new, unfamiliar and may even seem impossible. We are constantly searching for certainty in beliefs, ideas and the way we live our lives.

Over time we become blinkered to new ideas; we reinforce our beliefs and filter out anything that does not fit these beliefs, refusing to embrace the unexpected due to a fear of the unknown.

Look for ideas everywhere, particularly from the people around you. Remember that every individual on the planet is different and has had different experiences. It is important not to prejudge people who make seemingly strange suggestions. By considering all ideas as valid you will encourage the people around you to be more creative.

When you are out shopping, at a museum, the theatre or at home, look around you and seek inspiration from your surroundings. Real genius can come from the most unexpected sources.

Without the willingness to look at other possibilities, change won't occur, thoughts won't move forward, and problems will not be solved. Unless you are open to new ideas and thoughts, you will be stuck in a rut and never know what you're missing, or what might be possible. It is new ideas that move us forward, change us and offer us ways to reflect and learn.

In practice

- Try adopting a childlike approach and ask the seven whys – children ask why until they get to a point where they understand, or the parent gets frustrated and shuts them up! Using this approach may trigger new thoughts or ideas.

- Look for ideas in everything you see. Don't dismiss any ideas until you have had time to explore every possibility.

- Try combining ideas, bringing elements from disparate areas together.

- When someone comes up with what seems to be a strange idea, try to understand what is behind their thinking – take time to explore the idea. Have they had an experience that has coloured their thought process or do they have an insight which gives them a different viewpoint?

PLAN FOR ACTION

"To accomplish great things we must first dream, then visualise, then plan... believe... act!"

Alfred A. Montapert

The idea

Planning for action is a great catalyst for innovation. Having a clear vision of what you are trying, or going to achieve, with clear and understandable goals and strategies can galvanise you into action.

There is an old proverb: "He who fails to plan, plans to fail." This is so true when it comes to innovation. We are caught up in the excitement of creating something new or improving something that we forget to look at how things need to be implemented. I have worked with many large companies in both the UK and the US that celebrate the generation of ideas through suggestion schemes.

Similarly, there are companies that celebrate the registering of the greatest number of patents. One company I worked with had over 6,000 patents registered but was using less than 1% of them to make money. Although this is a noteworthy achievement, unless there are concrete plans to use the ideas or patents, their value to the organisation or society is negligible.

When we think about a new idea or solution, we need to think about how we can implement it. What will the roadmap be? What steps will we need to take to make it a reality?

If we look at the most innovative companies around the world, we will find that they not only talk about what they are going to do, but actually do it!

By planning for action it is likely that you will take that all-important first step, while if you just talk about it, it is probable that in 12 months you will still be talking about it. Nothing would have changed except for your level of frustration, and those around you would have become tired of listening to you talk about the same thing.

Once you have taken the first step, the second and third steps become much easier. When it is moving, a huge supertanker is easy to steer, while if it is stationary it takes many tugs to move. Similarly with innovative initiatives, once you are doing something it is easier to make progress towards your goal. You will not always get it right and you will have to make constant corrections to your plan, but there is progress.

Another story I like is that of the Apollo 13 space mission to the moon. The craft was apparently over 80% off-course on its journey to the moon, but the astronauts knew where the moon was and they could look out of the window and see where they were heading. They had a plan of how to get there, and a clear understanding of what success would look like, a first footstep on the moon surface.

So plan for action and take that all-important first step!

In practice

- One technique I have found particularly effective when planning for action is to roadmap the idea. Start at the end and assume that the idea has been implemented and is an incredible success. Work backwards and identify what steps you would have needed to take to get there.

Start thinking about not just that great idea, but what steps you would have to take to make it a reality.

Take some time to learn some rudimentary project management skills to help you break down your idea into manageable tasks.

When thinking about your plan, identify enabling and limiting factors that could affect the outcome of your initiative.

LIVE THE FUTURE

The idea

Many of us are caught up in the present which is safe and predictable. We can cope with thinking about the day, the week, next month and maybe even next year, particularly if we have a holiday or some other memorable event to look forward to. We may find it difficult to think five or ten years ahead as there are so many unknowns and uncertainties to consider. Trying to contemplate a world in the distant future may fall in the realm of science fiction for many of us. There is, however, real benefit in undertaking this kind of thinking as it can help us to create our own future.

An old proverb comes to mind: "Some people watch things happen, some people make things happen and some people wonder what the hell happened." If we do not plan for the future, we will be caught on the back foot and constantly find ourselves reacting to things that happen, wondering what the hell happened. By taking control of our future, we can influence the direction in which we move and what we are able to achieve.

Although thinking years in the future may seem like impossible it isn't that difficult if you try. The first thing to do is become aware of what is happening in the world. This may sound simple but with the pressures of daily life and our natural tendency to introverted thinking we sometimes forget to look around. A study by the Centre for Application of Psychological Type (CAPT) in the US estimated that in 2010 around 60% of Americans were introverted in their thinking.

Think about how events could change the future – unrest in the Arab nations, ageing population, economic factors, technology, etc. – and write down your thoughts about how these could play out.

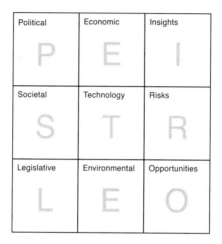

Figure 4: PESTLE Framework

The PESTLE framework may help focus your thinking in each of these areas.

Think about what would be different and how life would change. Create a view of how your world could be – it doesn't have to be accurate. In fact, chances are you will be wrong. It may be that there are a few possible future scenarios that will be determined by rising prices, scarcity of resources such as oil or gas, global warming and many other factors. The important thing is to keep your visualisation simple, don't over-complicate it or you will spend all your time over-analysing it.

The secret is to at least start thinking about possible alternate futures. You will be surprised by your ability to imagine. Once you have your future vision in place, think about what it would mean for you at home, at work and in your leisure time.

In practice

- Take time to write down what you think the future will be like. Don't worry about it being wrong as no one can accurately predict the future. Use it to understand what your problem/opportunity/idea would be like in this new world. Refer to the PESTLE framework to structure your thinking.

- Create three or four 'scenarios' set five years in the future. Make each one different by focusing on one factor in each case, such as climate, economy, social unrest and so on. Once you have your scenarios and alternate futures, look for what is common as well as what is different among them.

- Map out what each one would mean for you – think about the impact and the actions you might have to take.

- Finally, think about what you ideally would like to have in your future. Write it down and pin it to your notice board or some other prominent place, where you will be able to see it every day.

KEEP THINGS SIMPLE

"We are surrounded by engineers' follies; too many technical solutions still looking for problems to solve."

David Tansley

The idea

Human nature tends to overcomplicate things and the more information we have the more we try to analyse it. The Internet, although a great resource, has increased our ability to access information. Instead of a few books to browse, we now have millions of web pages from which to gather information.

K-I-S-S: Keep It Simple, Stupid. This mantra always pops into my head when I am looking at new ideas or solutions. The natural reaction is to keep adding features; other companies have been successful in the past, why not us? That is a bad idea. Too many new products and services are too complicated and tend to fail as a result.

An example of this is Microsoft. An average user 'needs' less than 5% of the functionality of programmes such as Word, Excel and PowerPoint. You can visualise the product teams coming up with lists of cool new features, and ending up with something that can be very daunting. In contrast, Apple's equivalent products are simple and give the user what they need, when they need it – a very different approach.

The French writer and poet Antoine de Saint Exupéry famously said, "It seems that perfection is reached not when there is nothing left to add, but when there is nothing left to take away." So, when you come up with that great idea or solution, take a step back and consider its practical aspect. What does the user or customer want or need? Can you make it simpler? Can you remove 'clutter'? The simpler solution is more likely to be understood and turned into reality.

By forcing ourselves to simplify things, we remove all the 'noise' that stops us from clearly seeing the reality.

In practice

- Look around you at the things you use every day. Can they be simplified or has someone already taken all the clutter out? How can they be improved?

- Think about a process that you do on a regular basis. It might be something at work or at home such as interacting with a bank, getting a vehicle serviced, preparing food, working with another company, etc. Map out all the steps in that process. Could some of them be removed? Is there something missing?

12 BRAND YOUR TEAM OR PROJECT

"Managing the beliefs of the organisation requires crafting a brand identity for creativity so it becomes part of the mentality and the expectations of everyone in the organisation."

John Kao

The idea

One of the secrets of innovation is that it is all about perception and permission. By creating a 'brand' for your team or project, you give focus, image and cohesion to all the activities you undertake.

Many large companies use this method to define their innovation activities, typically using a logo to signify that whatever is being presented or written about is part of an innovation initiative. This has the effect of differentiating it from other communication in the company.

Branding does not have to be complicated. It can be as simple as a particular colour of paper you use to communicate, or even a specific font. The brand communicates that you are dealing with innovation.

The brand should, if possible, reflect some element of the idea or solution. Here are a few examples of innovation brands from large companies and consultancies. From these examples, you can see that colour and metaphor are important as they give some sense of what the innovation activities are trying to do, be it leapfrogging over old ideas or creating a pathway to something new.

Figure 5: Idea Group Branding Examples

Ask your colleagues, family members and friends to suggest ideas. Be open to their thoughts and do not be judgmental.

Once you have your brand, use it on all your communication, on business cards, on email signatures – anywhere and on anything that is related to your innovation activity.

In practice

- Think about what you are trying to achieve with your idea or solution. Is it about implementing something new, changing something that exists, or perhaps a new way of doing something?

- Once you have an idea, think about what image or metaphor you could use. Be careful not to infringe copyright. It is worth doing a search on the Internet to see if anyone else has a trademark or is using a particular image that you want to use.

SPREAD THE WORD

"... what we are communicates far more eloquently than anything we say or do."

Stephen Covey

The idea

Effective communication is a key element of innovation. By spreading the word we give people 'permission' to be innovative, we also sell success and gain credibility from stakeholders, colleagues, team members and family.

Communication is not just verbal – our attitude, demeanour and enthusiasm are all part of how we spread the word. Remember that less than 15% of communication is what we say; the other 85% is our body language.

An important factor in successful innovation activities, whether at home or in the office, is the excitement and optimism that 'flows' around activities and people. This energy is infectious and good innovation activities often exhibit viral characteristics, triggering changes in behaviour not only in the people involved but also in those around them.

A great example of this is some work I did with a large government department in the UK that had been amalgamated with another department to save costs. I was using a technique developed by Jack Welch from General Electric in the US called Workout, which aims to engage teams in the job of innovating, and finding value and redundancy in what they do every day. The project was highly successful in its own right but what was more interesting was the culture change across the entire organisation. Those who were directly involved were going back to their day job enthusiastic, excited and fired-up. This enthusiasm and interest in doing things better spread to their colleagues and the benefit from the project ended up being four-fold.

Although communication is vital to an innovation activity, it is important that you have a plan about what and how you are going to communicate. Communicating things too early can raise expectations and interest which can falter if you don't deliver on time or give people what they expect. Getting your communication right can be the difference between success and failure in innovation.

Think carefully about what you want to get out of any communication. If it is to inform people then do it at the right time, if it is to enthuse them into innovative behaviour then it may be relevant to do it all the time.

In practice

Change your attitude – become more positive and enthusiastic and see what effect it has on your colleagues, friends and family.

Look for this behaviour in others, and encourage or perhaps even reward it.

Think about something you have done with people who are excited and enthusiastic. What effect did it have on you?

14 LOOK FOR THE SILVER LINING

The idea

We often focus on the negatives in life and this can lead us to dismiss ideas that may not be fully workable or complete. By forcing ourselves to look for the good in things, we have a greater chance of creating success.

We encounter obstacles throughout life and every time we fail, or don't get the result that we want, we dwell on the negative and admonish ourselves for making a mistake and not doing what we should have done, wishing for another outcome.

Taking this approach can be highly demoralising and have a potentially destructive impact on our lives. It can prevent us from taking action and trying something new.

This negative attitude can also lead to a blame culture that we see in many large organisations and even government bodies. Rather than seeing the positive, we focus on the negative and try to find somebody to blame for the unexpected outcome or uncomfortable situation. You only have to listen to the news on the radio or TV to find examples of how we focus on the negative. How many 'good news' items do you hear about?

Rather than focus on the negative, look for the positive aspects of a situation – what have you learnt, what would you do differently, how could something positive be made out of it? Don't say "I wish I had done …" instead say "… next time this is what I will do!"

Beating yourself up about the past is going to get you nowhere. By finding the positive in every situation, you are taking control of your life and preparing for the future.

In practice

- Take an everyday situation that has a negative outcome. Write down a brief description at the top of a sheet of paper and then write down a list of all the positives you can think of. Then turn the sheet over and write down all the negatives – by the side of each negative write a positive.

- Look for the positive in everything – take a newspaper article or a news item on the TV, which on the surface seems negative, and write down five positive things about it.

- If somebody comes to you with a problem, ask them to tell you three positive things about it or three ways that it can be built on.

- One technique to consider is Appreciative Inquiry which was developed in the US in the early 1980s. This approach, which focuses on looking at the positive in any situation and building on it for a desired outcome, is particularly pertinent for change initiatives in organisations.

PART 2

CREATIVITY & IDEAS

Personal innovation and creativity are more important than ever. There is a desperate need for people who see things differently, who can size up problems quickly and develop creative solutions. There are thousands of tools and techniques that can be used; which one is right will depend on you as an individual, and the environment you operate in.

THE 20:20:20 TECHNIQUE

"You cannot open a book without learning something."

Confucius

The idea

One of the main obstacles to innovation is often just finding ideas, unmet needs, problems and opportunities on which to focus your thinking. There are many techniques in this book that will help you, and there are also thousands of websites offering tools, techniques and guidance. Find what works for you and what provides you with the most stimulation.

Many tools and techniques focus on generating ideas, few seem to focus on finding the problem first. Once the problem or unmet need is identified, it is easier to come up with solutions and ideas.

I developed a technique to find subjects for blog posts on my website. Key to successful blogging is to keep your readers interest alive by posting regularly. Finding things to blog about can be a problem at times. So I would go into a bookshop, library or newsagent and look through 20 magazines for 20 minutes, and try to come up with 20 ideas for new blog posts.

I found this technique worked very well and I started using it to generate ideas for products and services for the company I was working for. I used my knowledge of the capabilities, skills and possibilities within the company along with the random stimulation of magazines, books and newspaper articles to find links and insights into new things we could do.

This technique helps you spot opportunities or problems that are current as it gathers ideas from the latest magazines, newspapers or the Internet. Once you get used to the technique you will find yourself looking for problems and opportunities wherever you are, at home watching television, while seated in a restaurant or a train, or even while just walking down the street.

One important thing to remember when applying this technique is to make sure you have some way of recording your ideas – a notebook, voice recorder, phone, post-it notes – anything that will act as a reminder of your idea or solution.

A downside, however, is that if you are using a newsagent or a bookstore, you will need to constantly find new ones since the staff can get annoyed if you just go in and read for 20 minutes without buying anything!

In practice

- 20:20:20 is an idea-generating technique I find most useful and one that you can practice almost anywhere. Find a place with a pile of magazines or newspapers and browse through a few. I like to say 20 but it doesn't have to be that many. Then sit down for 20 minutes, quickly scan through them for interesting articles or headlines and write down 20 problems or opportunities you find.

- Write down an idea or solution for each problem or opportunity. Once you have your list look for commonalities or linkages and rewrite the list. Lastly, prioritise them based on the ease of implementation and impact they could have. You now have a list of great ideas or solutions to current problems!

- Try the same technique with books in a library or use the 'random' button on Google search.

- Have a go at the technique the next time you are at the dentist, the doctor's, or at a car garage. One interesting observation I have made using this technique is that your environment colours what you think. Is this true for you?

16 | USING 8:3:3 – FINDING YOUR PASSION!

"If there is no passion in your life, then have you really lived? Find your passion, whatever it may be. Become it, and let it become you and you will find great things happen FOR you, TO you and BECAUSE of you."

T. Allan Armstrong

The idea

One of the drivers of innovation is passion for an idea, a need, a problem or an untapped opportunity. Many of the greatest ideas are fueled by passion, be it Google and their passion for information, Apple and their passion for design, or Virgin and their passion for customer service. All these passions have driven disruptive innovation in their chosen sector, often creating significant value while shaping the market.

Understanding your particular passion is the starting point; for some this will be easy, for others it will be a challenge.

As children we have many interests and passions, it may be a television programme, a toy, a series of books or a pop group. The good thing about these childhood passions is that they usually change as we get older and we find new things to be passionate about. Sometimes these early passions may continue into adulthood, but often as we get older, we become focused on a single passion, something that becomes a key part of our lives and can define us. When you hear someone talk about his or her passion, you can sense the excitement and energy in them.

What defines a passion? The word passion is derived from the Ancient Greek verb πάσχω (paskho), which means to suffer or to endure. It is an intense emotion compelling feeling, enthusiasm or desire for something. The term is also often applied to a lively or eager interest in, or admiration for, a proposal, cause or activity.

Passion is probably the most important factor in the success of any project, business venture or activity. It is a key aspect that drives people to succeed; a lack of it is one of the main causes of failure. It is interesting that when small successful ventures are taken to initial public offering (IPO) or acquired by larger companies, the founder usually leaves with a massive package and all the value in the company dies – the passion has gone, the vision has clouded. Studies reveal that approximately 40% to 80% of mergers and acquisitions prove to be disappointing.

To be a successful innovator, it is important that you find the project, solution or idea that fires your passion and fills your mind day and night. The sad thing is that few people find their passion in what they do to earn an income, relying instead on activities and interests outside their working life. The secret is to turn this enthusiasm and energy for something you do every day into a way of earning a living.

The moment you find your passion can be one of the most wonderful of your life. Doing what you love will lead you to success and to the perception of success. You will achieve more, and you will feel happier and more fulfilled than ever before.

In practice

- Take a sheet of blank paper and write down eight things you are passionate about. These can be related to something at home, at work, a project, hobby or anything else. Alongside each write down three reasons why you are passionate about the item. Lastly, write a separate list of the three things that link these passions.

- Once you have your lists, use them as a 'lens' to look for interesting areas to innovate in. When you are reading the newspaper, magazine or the Internet, look for opportunities to explore your passion.

- Find the passion in others – they could well provide you with insights into a possible area for innovation.

HAVE FUN!

"The joy is in creating, not maintaining."

Vince Lombardi

The idea

Some of our best ideas come when we are having fun. Play often brings out the child in us and we forget our inhibitions and restrictive beliefs. As children we were open to everything around us. We were curious, we wanted to learn about our world. Small children make up fantastic stories with their toys, creating new worlds for their toys to exist in, and spinning tales about their activities.

As we get older, we continue to have this intrinsic ability, but many of us choose to suppress or ignore it, hiding it from the world. We become serious and we develop a 'need' to belong to the society we live in, therefore we conform to its values, beliefs and norms. This move to conformity removes the curiosity we had as children, replacing it with the certainties we are taught in school, at home and in our working environment.

Although the acceptance of these certainties allows us to be part of the world we live in, innovation sometimes comes from challenging these certainties, finding new ways to do things and new insights.

"Aha! is only one letter away from ha-ha."

Howard Wright

One of the key things I have discovered from working in innovation for almost two decades is the role of fun and laughter in releasing some of the latent curiosity and creativity that lies in all of us.

Laughter also breaks down social and hierarchical barriers that exist in groups. It is an effective leveler, a way of connecting people at a subliminal level and of removing tensions and diffusing conflicts. Research in the US in the late 1990s suggests that even while on the telephone, people you are communicating with can detect whether you are smiling.

The benefits of laughter are numerous:

- Laughing releases endorphins which boost your immune system and stimulate the lymphatic system. It reduces stress in minutes and you get ill less often.

- It gives you a natural feel-good high. Have you noticed how a long, hard laugh gives you an emotional release that leaves you feeling revitalised? That warm feeling you get from laughing also creates a positive attitude, putting problems in perspective and enabling you to tackle them more calmly. It works your diaphragm as well as a number of key muscle groups!

- Laughing nourishes your brain and helps keep it alert and active. It also stimulates both sides of the brain and can improve your ability to retain information.

How many times have you walked into an office and noticed people laughing and having fun? Probably not many. We tend to be dour and solemn at our workplaces and we wonder why we don't enjoy our jobs and why we are not more creative. I am not advocating anarchy in the office but having fun should be part of our everyday working lives.

Encourage innovation and curiosity... start finding the funny side of life, change your demeanour and, most importantly, have fun!

In practice

To understand the power of laughter, try writing a list of ideas around a particular topic, for example, 'Things you could do with a toothbrush'. Then do the same thing while watching a funny movie, TV programme, or listening to a comedy on the radio. See what the effect is on the content and quantity of your ideas.

Set aside 'funny time' each day. Why not use some of your break time to read a comic or joke book?

Dedicate time in the office to a fun hour or to play a game. This might seem strange but it is a great way to find out things about your colleagues and to generate team spirit.

One of my colleagues used to organise Nintendo Wii bowling competitions at lunch with teams competing against each other. Unfortunately, it was stopped as it generated too much laughter, and there were objections to the noise. But the productivity of those involved went up notably in the afternoons, and their energy levels increased significantly.

Smile. By doing so you not only exercise many muscles in your face but you also change your demeanour and the way people view you – don't forget that 85% of communication is non-verbal.

HEROES AND VILLAINS

> "Stories are the creative conversion of life itself into a more powerful, clearer, more meaningful experience. They are the currency of human contact."

> Robert McKee

The idea

Stories are a powerful way of organising and sharing individual experiences, as well as exploring and creating shared realities. They form an underlying structure of society and a way of passing culture on to others, be it corporate culture or the foundation of the society we live in. They tell us what is acceptable, what we can do and what we can't do.

Too few business leaders grasp the idea that stories can positively impact the people around them. Leaders who understand this and use the power of stories to help grow their organisations, are the ones who are successful. Those who fail to grasp or use the power of stories miss the opportunity to shape and change the world around them. Stories speak to an inner self; they help us better understand our world, our lives and ourselves.

When I was researching my last book, I interviewed Alan Leighton, then Chair of Royal Mail. He told me a story of when he worked at the confectionary company Mars. He was a junior manager and was sent to the Maltesers (small round chocolate honeycomb sweets) production line to learn about the procedure. He was given a brush and shovel and told to sweep up the chocolates that had fallen on the floor. Being round, the chocolates rolled around and he spent the first hour chasing them, getting very few onto his shovel. After an hour, the supervisor took pity on him and showed him that rather than chase the chocolates around, if he stepped on them first and crushed them, they were easier to sweep up. The story, although seemingly trivial, provides a lesson in that you need to be open to other people's ideas and knowledge, and that when you are in somebody else's space, take advantage of their expertise!

Stories can be an effective way of communicating with potential customers. Not only does this form of communication make the idea or problem understandable, it also lets you introduce humour into the situation, which can help get people's creative juices flowing. Having heroes and villains is one way of putting forward ideas about who you need to help you (the heroes), and who might try to stop you (the villains).

There are many books that deal with the subject of storytelling and provide 'formal' structures for creating stories. The most famous is the 'Heroes' Journey'. Try using the storytelling worksheet below to create your own story.

In practice

- Assume that you have solved your problem or exploited the opportunity for innovation. Who were the heroes and villains you met on the way? Which characters helped you and how did they do it? Who tried to stop you and how did you overcome them? Draw insights from this and use it to help define your strategy for success.

Heroes
Villians
Helpers
Situation
What barriers did the hero have to overcome?
What was the result?
The moral of the story is...
What insight did you gain?

Figure 6: Storytelling Worksheet

- Write a story that explains what life would be like if you had been successful. Set it five years into the future. Again, who helped you and who tried to stop you?

- Write a dialogue between two people, one of whom has benefitted from your idea.

- Think about someone who has benefitted from your innovation. Who are their heroes and villains?

19 BE CHILDLIKE, NOT CHILDISH

"Great is the human who has not lost his childlike heart."

Mencius (Meng-Tse), 4th century BCE

The idea

When we are young, we have a natural curiosity and we constantly ask 'why'. Although this can be extremely annoying for parents and teachers, it is a sign of our intense interest in the world around us and our fascination with everything we see, hear and touch.

As we grow older, we lose the ability to question, and we assume we know the answers. We lose the natural wonder and curiosity we had as children.

Great innovators rediscover the childlike curiosity and attitude to risk that makes them different from people around them. They learn to look at things in new ways, to see things that others don't see, and to question what they don't understand.

One technique that often helps tap into our hidden creative capabilities is play. In the 1990s, Lego started using its own product to help senior management teams become more creative. This was so successful that they launched it as a service to other companies – called Lego Serious Play – now available through a range of franchised consultancy companies around the world.

Although the 'formal' process they developed is highly effective, you don't need to spend huge amounts of money to use this technique. Lego is readily available at most toy shops and you can buy a basic kit.

Use the blocks to build a representation of the problem or need you are trying to resolve, and then adapt the blocks to represent your idea or solution to a problem. Don't be put off if it seems silly, that is part of the technique. Ask your family, friends or trusted colleagues to build their version of how they see your idea and get them to tell you the story about why they built what they did and what it represents. If you find it useful and want to learn more, check out the Lego Serious Play website at www.seriousplay.com.

In some of my previous workshops, when I introduced toys to add colour and stimulation, I found that when people picked them up and played with them they became more creative in their contribution to the workshop or in their work. When I spoke to a psychologist many months later, he shared that through play we were in fact tapping into a time before our self-limiting belief system was fully formed, and psychologically relocating ourselves in our childhood.

Becoming childlike in our approach to a problem or situation can open our minds to new thoughts and ideas. Introducing play into the creative process can also bring humour and fun, both of which are key elements of innovation, into it.

In practice

- Buy yourself some Lego and have a go at using the blocks to create models that represent the problem or need you are trying to address, and explain how your idea is going to solve it.

- Ask family and friends to build models which represent your idea or solution. Get them to tell you the story of why they built what they did and you might be surprised at what they tell you.

- Get some toys for your work environment. They don't have to be expensive with stores such as Ikea stocking a variety of cheap, stimulating items. Buy a few and rotate them so you have something new to play with each week.

20 GENERATE AS MANY IDEAS AS YOU CAN

"Creativity, as has been said, consists largely of rearranging what we know in order to find out what we do not know. Hence to think creatively we must be able to look afresh at what we already know."

George Kneller

The idea

The more ideas you have, the more likely you are to produce one successful one. In large organisations, the success rate of idea generation and innovation schemes is between 2% – 5%. This means that over 95% of ideas fail to generate value for the organisation. This percentage is probably higher for an individual as you will often filter out the more radical ideas that tend to be captured in group situations.

Try as many different techniques as you can to generate ideas – some may work better for one type of person than others. There are a few in this book but a quick search on the Internet will reveal many hundreds. Use a variety of techniques to look at the same problem and think about what worked and what didn't. What does this tell you about how you like to work?

Idea generation should not be a one-off activity; it should be something that you do all the time. Train yourself to continually think about things around you, look for opportunities, try to identify problems and find unmet needs around you.

Remember to have a strategy for capturing your ideas, whether on a piece of paper, a Dictaphone or your mobile phone. Ideas can come to you at any time so keep a notepad by your bed, in your car, maybe even in the bathroom! Ideas tend not to linger and can be quickly replaced with the next one so it is important to capture your thoughts 'in the moment' rather than wait half an hour until you find something to write on.

There are differing views on whether idea generation is a solitary or group activity, so try both approaches and see what works for you. Some people like to talk through their ideas and therefore work better in a group situation, while others prefer to generate ideas themselves and then work them through a group.

When you have a noteworthy idea, it is good to commit it to paper at some point as this gives you the opportunity to visualise and think about it. Once you have it written down, look at how you can build on it. Be careful though as some of the best ideas are the simplest!

In practice

- Set aside an 'idea time' every week. Go somewhere with the objective of generating ideas – this could be a coffee shop or somewhere more stimulating such as an art gallery or a museum. Plan to come away with at least 20 ideas.

- Try generating ideas on a particular topic in a solitary manner and then try the same exercise in a group environment.

- Keep a record of all your ideas. A simple Excel spreadsheet is a great way of recording them. Assign a category to each idea and what you need to make it happen. This will allow you to sort through the ideas later.

- Find a way of capturing ideas, possibly a journal, and make sure that you have access to it 24 hours a day – some of the best ideas occur at 4am!

- Try different techniques on the same problem. You could even use a different style of technique every month.

READ SCIENCE FICTION

"Companies fail to create the future, not because they fail to predict it but because they fail to imagine it."

Gary Hammel

The idea

The science fiction genre encompasses some of the most creative and innovative writing and can be a great source for new ideas. Many academic and research establishments use science fiction, either consciously or unconsciously, to guide their work. Television shows such as *Star Trek* have influenced the production of mobile phones and other industries, and scientists are still working on Tricorders for medical diagnostics. The iPhone is perhaps the closest we have come to the *Star Trek* communicator and while we are still waiting for the transporter, a cloaking device or a holodeck... I believe it will just be a matter of time before it is in use.

Innovation happens when we refuse to accept what we have today and instead imagine an alternative reality. The beauty of fiction, and especially science fiction, is that it is not just about specific advanced technologies, it also introduces an imagined social context for these technologies.

Science fiction can serve as a kind of forward-looking history; it introduces us to an imagined world and its technologies, that may one day become our reality. It also forces us to consider the implications of alternate futures and to question whether this is a path we want to follow.

Arthur C. Clarke, one of the greatest science fiction writers of our time, was a master of innovation. His 1979 book *The Fountains of Paradise* describes a space elevator based on a cable system tethered at the Earth's equator which rises to the point where the system's centre of gravity maintains a geostationary orbit. This provides a platform for electric cars running up and down the cable, negating the need for rocket launches as the cars can carry spacecraft out of the earth's gravitational field. At the time this was unthinkable, but several US startups are now trying to design such a 'space elevator'. Clarke's novel specified amazing detail, including the use of crystalline carbon fibre for the cable and 'spider' construction methods, which are elements of some of the attempts today.

What science fiction writing does is that it allows us to imagine a future without the constraints of today. We can create a world without boundaries, or different ones at least. It frees the imagination and provides a platform for our wildest dreams.

"The connection is so profound that it comes down to the only difference between science fiction and science is timing. Every generation imagines something they want to do and can't do, so they write about it. That inspires the kids so that to go and accomplish it, they develop the technologies and the engineering toolset.

When you have the advantage of hindsight, it's rather staggering how much of what we do today is last generation's science fiction."

Dean Kamen, inventor of the Segway

However, science fiction doesn't always get it right and you have to use your own judgment as to its probability and effect. It does, however, provide an interesting challenge on the art of the possible... the trick is to convert it into the science of the practical!

In practice

- Read a new science fiction book every month for three months and see if this brings any new insights. When you have finished each book write down any insights or ideas you have.

- Write down one of your opportunities or problems and then watch an episode of *Star Trek* – is there anything in the episode that triggers an insight into your idea?

- Try writing your own science fiction story that incorporates your idea or solution. Set it far in the future and maybe on a distant planet.

  - How would the problem or need manifest itself in this new setting and how would it be solved?

  - Who would the characters be and how would they behave?

  - What would the outcome be?

- Lastly, what did you learn from this exercise?

LOOK BACK AT HISTORY

"Those who refuse to learn from history are condemned to repeat it."

George Santayana

The idea

Not every problem is new. There is a strong possibility that someone in the past has dealt with the issue before you, or the opportunity you face. It might not be exactly the same but there will be strong parallels.

History does repeat itself, never exactly, but it shows us patterns of thinking. If you look back at life in Pompeii in 79AD, it is not very different, in essence, from what we see today. Of course, we have more technology now, but the fundamental day-to-day life shares strong similarities.

People back then often faced the same challenges that we do today, although the context and technology are different. Having fewer resources and experience meant that they had to be innovative and find new ways of doing things, similar to people in parts of Africa and India today where a 'make do and mend' attitude forces them to be innovative.

Another source of great innovation is conflict. During the various wars around the world, particularly the First and Second World Wars, there was tremendous innovation – again sparked by a burning need coupled with a lack of available resources.

We not only need to learn from history, so we don't repeat the same mistakes, we also need to look to history for inspiration. One of the key factors of innovation is not only having great ideas but also having the right conditions for them to come alive and survive. What was a great idea 50 years ago may not have been practical then as the environment wasn't right. Today things may have changed and it could be that this same idea could change the world.

Another source of inspiration is art, such as the works by Leonardo Da Vinci, Rembrandt or even Hieronymus Bosch. Although these are not going to give you a direct link to history, they will give you some inspiration.

Looking back at what 'has been' is a fascinating pastime although it should not become your only source of inspiration. Use this technique to find new ideas and insights instead of trawling through endless websites and books.

Just as environmental conditions may have had an impact on past ideas, similarly, they may also be affected by a variety of other factors beyond your control, so keep a database of your ideas to save them for use later. I use a basic Excel spreadsheet to record my ideas and I revisit it on a regular basis to see if an idea I had a year ago could 'fly' today.

In practice

- Spend some time on the Internet and search for examples which align with your problems or opportunities.

- Set up a database to catalogue your ideas – plan to spend an hour a month revisiting your ideas.

- Visit the local art gallery and spend some time looking at the paintings and sculptures.

- Look to Patents databases to find possible inspiration. (www.google.com/patents is a great place to start.)

- Read about the way people overcame problems in the First and Second World Wars, keeping your problem or opportunity in mind. Are there linkages between your problem and how people solved theirs in the past?

- Try resource constraining yourself as your ancestors did. If you didn't have access to all the resources you needed what would you do? How would you do things differently? How would the Romans have solved your problem or fulfilled your unmet need?

MEDIA STORMING

"The creative person wants to be a know-it-all. He wants to know about all kinds of things: ancient history, nineteenth-century mathematics, current manufacturing techniques, flower arranging, and hog futures. Because he never knows when these ideas might come together to form a new idea. It may happen six minutes later or six months, or six years down the road. But he has faith that it will happen."

Carl Ally

The idea

Expand your reading to new and diverse media sources. Once you have articulated your problem or situation take a random newspaper, magazine, book, TV programme or website and focus on one headline, chapter, article, etc. Force yourself to read things that you wouldn't normally be interested in and you may find a solution to your problem, or a way to make your idea work.

The more stimulation you can gain from diverse media sources, the more chance you will have of finding that all-important linkage between your problem and a solution. Innovation is all about creating linkages; often between seemingly disparate ideas or situations, so the more you can expose yourself to these the better it is.

When you read a magazine, a book, a newspaper or an article on the Internet, keep your problem or idea at the back of your mind. Constantly look for possible linkages between what you are reading and your idea – even if the link is tenuous, write it down. It may just be the insight you are looking for.

The secret to this technique is to constantly look for ideas in the media. The more you use this technique, the more insight you will gain and the easier it will become to gain inspiration.

You will find that you start to get ideas from all around you – TV, advertising posters, overhearing a conversation on a train, even on junk mail! You will start to build linkages between seemingly disparate information which is the basis of great innovation.

The more media you are exposed to the more likely you are to find that all important insight or linkage. Keep an open and inquisitive mind and constantly look for ideas and insights.

In practice

- Buy at least one magazine or newspaper that you would not buy on a weekly basis. Take time to read it and see if there is something in it that helps with one of your problems or ideas.

- Dentists and doctors usually have a good supply of interesting magazines; use the waiting time to generate some ideas.

- Try to reverse the technique by picking a random article and come up with an idea or solution that is radical, something that has never been tried before.

- Use Google's random page function to see if it provides new insights into your idea.

- Ask your friends and family to provide you with magazines, newspapers and books that may help provide some stimulation for ideas.

24 BIOMIMICRY – HOW WOULD NATURE DO IT?

"A bird doesn't sing because it has an answer, it sings because it has a song."

Lou Holtz

The idea

We have been surrounded by biomimicry for the last 37 million years; it has been around longer than we humans. Biomimicry is the idea of using nature to inspire design and engineering by learning from organisms, plants and animals. Evolution is also an interesting factor when considering nature as stimulation for innovation. The natural selection process focuses on the elements of life that ensure survival – the things that are important in the environment that the creature or plant is in.

Architects, designers and engineers are becoming increasingly interested in nature and biologists are becoming involved in a whole range of projects from building design to software, business and strategy.

This isn't something new and we have seen nature play its part in technology over the past 5 – 10 years with systems such as Neural Networks mimicking the way we think the brain works, software that protects itself using techniques developed from the human immune system, to buildings that cool themselves the same way that ants cool their nests.

Current research in warfare is looking at creating flying machines the size of insects, with cameras and sensors on board. Another example is the Speedo wet suits created for Olympic swimmers that mimic the skin of a shark and provide a more efficient flow through the water.

Taking this to the next stage would mean that in a biomimetic world, we would manufacture things the way plants and animals do, using the sun and simple compounds to produce totally biodegradable fibres, ceramics, plastics, and chemicals.

So, when you are faced with a particular problem or opportunity, spend some time exploring the world around you. Think about how nature would solve this particular problem. Become more aware of the world around you and look for solutions not on the Internet or in books, but in your garden or in the countryside.

The more our ideas and solutions 'mimic' the natural world the more likely they are to be unique and show value. Nature has a way of simplifying things, only needing what is necessary.

In practice

- Once you have identified your problem or opportunity, visit a natural history museum and look for inspiration and ideas in the exhibits there.

- Think about how nature would solve the particular problem or address the opportunity. Is there a natural approach, maybe an ant's nest or the skin of a fish that might work? Think laterally not linearly.

- Don't always focus on the bigger picture, look to the macro world and focus on the detail of how nature structures itself. Can you gain insights at this level? There are many highly detailed photographs taken with electron microscopes on the Internet – find one and see if you can gain any insight or linkages with your problem.

- Use the Internet to seek out ideas from nature. Search out possible insights from nature websites such as the BBC Nature site.

MAKE THINGS LOOK RIDICULOUS… ON PURPOSE

25

> *"Do something. If it doesn't work, do something else. No idea is too crazy."*
>
> Jim Hightower

The idea

We see the world as we have always seen it, through the same eyes and with the same preconceptions. Although this is fine for much of the time, when we want to change things or come up with a new way of seeing something it can hold us back and keep us in our safety zone.

When we make things ridiculous, either physically or mentally, we start to see things differently, to challenge our embedded beliefs and preconceptions. Laughter stimulates endorphins, boosting our brain activity and, hopefully, generating new ideas and insights.

To create a killer idea, you need to drop your prejudice of what "sounds right" and create ideas that will most likely sound stupid. The next time you hear a stupid idea, catch yourself from immediately dismissing it and ask if you are applying "old think". Recognising your own biases is the way to transition from being creatively boring to becoming a true innovator.

Give yourself permission to be silly – embrace the odd, the zany and those stupid ideas that pop into your head before you quickly dismiss them as too ridiculous. There may just be a gem in there. Go on, give it a go!

Note: Try not to laugh out loud as you will get some strange looks; though it can be a way of breaking the ice at conferences, you may end up trying to explain why you imagined the speaker dressed as a banana! One approach is that of *Chindogu*, a Japanese word coined for the art of the unuseless idea. These strangely practical and utterly eccentric inventions took Japan by storm in the 1980s when amateur inventor Kenji Kawakami discovered a not-quite usable idea for a new gadget.

In practice

- Take an everyday situation and turn it around in your mind to make it ridiculous. It may be that you put someone in a strange situation, or changed the colour or texture of something to make it funny. Imagine how things would be different for the people around you, how would they react?

- When thinking about a particular problem you are facing, try turning things upside down, make the serious things funny.

- Check out some of the *Chindogu* innovations and see if they provide any insight into your problem. If you were going to solve your problem using *Chindogu* principles, what would you do? Ask your colleagues, friends and family to come up with their ideas.

26 STOP TELLING YOURSELF YOU'RE NOT INNOVATIVE

"All human development, no matter what form it takes, must be outside the rules; otherwise we would never have anything new."

Charles Kettering

The idea

If you tell yourself that you will not be able to come up with ideas, then you probably will not, no matter how hard you try. We are 'slaves' to our own belief systems that we have built up over our lives. These beliefs are usually based on our experiences, stories about other people and our preconceptions of reality. Often this self-limiting belief system stops us from becoming amazing.

We need to get out of our own way!

We end up working our entire lives to develop skills and knowledge that allow us to succeed but we may become so competent that we stop ourselves from being innovative. We think we know the answer because we have seen this particular situation before, but in reality these learned behaviours and perceptions could be holding us back from being creative. They are good in certain situations, for instance, when you are dealing with the familiar or when there is a defined process to follow. They are great when you are in some kind of danger – if there is a snarling lion charging towards you it is good to believe that you need to run! If things aren't working or if there is an opportunity to improve things through innovation, these old patterns of behaviour and beliefs can be detrimental to creating new ideas and solutions.

Don't shut your innovative thought process down by criticising and over analysing the ideas that do come to you. Tell yourself that you have great ideas. Allow yourself to imagine and dream up ideas freely like children do. Let the inner child in you out – forget all the cannots, buts and should nots that we absorb everyday and let your thoughts flow freely.

When you come up with an idea, however crazy it is, pat yourself on the back, smile and tell yourself that it is a brilliant idea! Don't forget to write it down so you don't forget it. It might not be the best idea that you have ever had, but it may be the link in the chain that allows an improved idea to form.

So, get out of your own way, listen and look at the world with an open mind. Tell yourself that you are the most innovative person you know. You can succeed at anything you try to do, you cannot fail.

In practice

- Take time to write down all your accomplishments. This will help you realise what you have achieved in your life so far.

- The next time you have an idea write it down and think about how you can make it happen. Tell yourself how good you are and what a creative idea it was, rather than focusing on all the problems that could arise.

CARRY A CAMERA

"The camera doesn't make a bit of difference. All of them can record what you are seeing. But, you have to SEE."

Ernst Haas

The idea

Our lives are so busy that we often don't see what is around us. Our surroundings become so familiar that we may only notice the things that have changed. This behaviour is our brain's way of filtering out the normal and only responding to the abnormal or what has changed around us.

Creativity is seen as an activity of the 'right brain' or the visual cortex, which is the side of the brain that processes images. Though it is referred to as the right brain, the visual cortex is actually at the back of the brain. In our working lives most of us tend to dismiss our right brain, our creative side, and focus on our left brain, our logical side.

This left side dominance leads to the analysis of everything we think and do. Often stopping us from being innovative, or if we are, it is likely to be incremental rather than any radical form of innovation. Unfortunately, this tendency towards analysis is often what business and society values on a day-to-day basis.

My own personal view is that 'true' innovation is about learning to use your brain in balance; the right side to create the ideas and the left side to structure and implement them. This is not rocket science and by applying and trying some of the ideas in this book, you will start to find the balance. The more you force yourself to use both sides of the brain, the easier it will become.

Innovative people are endlessly curious about the world around them. They observe the world, ask questions, and then see what they can do to make the world a better place, or work out how they can benefit from apparent and real 'market failures'.

By being alert throughout the day, rather than operating on autopilot, you will see things in a new light. Things that have always been there will suddenly be brought into sharp focus. The texture of buildings, the colours of trees and plants, the sounds of daily life are all possible sources of ideas and insights. Having your eyes and mind open will help you see, feel and hear the numerous opportunities there are to be innovative all day, every day.

One technique that works really well, and forces us to actually take in a particular scene, is to take a picture of something. Don't just take pictures of the unusual but take pictures of things you see every day. Try taking them from a different angle, or take a close up image rather than a typical 'holiday photo'.

Images conjure up emotions within us. When we look at a picture we have taken, often we can remember how we felt at that moment, as well as the temperature, sounds and smells associated with the memory.

By carrying a camera and recording things around us we are capturing these moments which can later be used to illustrate an idea, to trigger inspiration, to recall a thought or just to rekindle a memory of an event.

Historically, the cost of photography was high, but with the arrival and proliferation of digital cameras and camera phones, the opportunity to take many pictures is high and the cost almost zero!

In practice

- Set a quota for photos and force yourself to take them. Don't go to new places but instead force yourself to find new perspectives on old situations. You probably hadn't noticed that crack in the pavement before, the decoration on a particular building, the texture on the bark of a tree or the colours and detail of a flower.

- Take a close-up photo of something and study it. Most digital cameras today have a macro mode that allows you to get up close and personal with the subject. Try using this to study an everyday object in a new way.

- When you are faced with a problem or opportunity, try searching for an image related to it on Google. See what comes up – is there anything here that can provide a new insight?

28 LISTEN TO CLASSICAL MUSIC

"He who hears music, feels his solitude peopled at once."

Robert Browning

The idea

Listening to any music can be relaxing and therapeutic as it has the effect of temporarily clearing our minds of clutter. We forget all our problems and concentrate on what we are hearing. There have been a number of research studies that have concluded that music has positive effects on the human brain. Giving ourselves time and space to listen to classical music allows our subconscious mind to concentrate on whatever issue we are facing, or opportunities we have identified. It prevents the mind from being stuck in a rut and provides continuous stimulation.

Although we can achieve this 'disconnection' with any music, the technique has proved most efficacious with classical music – particularly Bach and Mozart. The type of music that we listen to has a significant influence on our performance and bodily response.

As human beings, we are primitively affected by music because of its rhythm. Our bodies have their own natural rhythm, found in our heartbeat, our breathing, how we walk and even blink. It is natural that we respond to the rhythm of music around us and align our rhythm to that in the music we are listening to – slowing down or speeding up according to the rise and fall of the musical beats. Classical music causes the heartbeat and pulse rate to relax.

When the body is relaxed, the mind is able to concentrate better. Furthermore, it has been proven that classical music decreases blood pressure and enhances the ability to learn. Music also has an impact on the amplitude and frequency of brain waves measured by an electroencephalogram and affects the breathing rate and the electrical resistance of the skin.

The Mozart effect

A study conducted by a French researcher, Dr. Alfred A. Tomatis, and published in his 1991 book *Pourquoi Mozart?*, found that listening to Mozart promoted healing and the development of the brain. Another study in 1993 by Shaw Rauscher, found that listening to Mozart helped with 'spatial intelligence' although it also showed that the enhancing effect of the music was only temporary.

Although there are differing views on the benefits of classical and other types of music, the sheer act of sitting down and listening is enough to provide you with the time and space to think. If the music helps to stimulate ideas, it's even better.

In practice

Set aside some time during your week to sit down and listen to some classical music – maybe Bach or Mozart. The best way, I have found, is to sit in a quiet room with a pair of headphones so that external distractions are removed and I can fully become attuned to the rhythms and repetitions of the music.

29 BE A VISITOR IN YOUR OWN WORLD

"The world really boils down to two kinds of people: those that see shapes in cloud formations, and those that just see clouds."

Danzai Pace

The idea

There are days where things just seem dull, weird and out of sync. You feel at a loss and out of sorts, just not in the mood to listen to music or to read a book! We tend to get into a rut sometimes with the mundaneness of our daily lives – when we travel to work in the same way, we go to the same office and do the same things. If we follow this pattern it is going to be hard to think differently!

Familiarity breeds contempt and if you do the same things every day, you are bound to get the same outcomes.

"Insanity: doing the same thing over and over again and expecting different results."

Albert Einstein

There are a number of 'tricks' you can use to snap out of this mood. Your environment is an important factor in how well you work, and more importantly, how effectively you think. Even if you have an exceptional setting, it can get stale if you see it every day. The familiar can become invisible.

To get out of this situation you need to change things around, create a new environment, a new place to work.

One trick is to rearrange your office. Move your desk, switch your pictures around, try different lighting if you can.

What works well for me is to change where I work. This can be achieved by moving my chair to the other side of the desk or maybe trading offices or desks with someone else.

If you have the flexibility, find a new environment to work in. When I was writing this book I found that I couldn't work in my home office anymore, as I was not motivated by the environment. I kept getting writer's block. So I sought out a new, more stimulating environment and moved my office, for an hour or so each morning, to a local coffee shop. The buzz, the chatter and the bustle of the place helped block out any problems or issues I might have had, and new ideas and concepts just flowed. I have even been known to park my car in my favourite spot, roll down the windows and work for a while.

Changing your surroundings helps to change the way you think and ultimately to change who you are. Your environment is an important part of your identity, and in some respects, defines who you are. Every day it reinforces your perceptions of yourself and how you think. Change your environment and make it stimulating and it will help reinforce a new way of thinking. Even changing what you wear can make a difference. This way you can start the journey to become the person you want to be.

It is easy to stick with the familiar, there is security in certainty, but try some of these things out and I guarantee you will notice the difference. Your environment, and particularly your perspective on it, greatly affects how and what you do.

In practice

- Sit in the guest chair on the opposite side of your desk for an hour or so. It will give you a fresh perspective on the same old environment. Even the slightest change in your physical setting can stimulate your senses and your creativity. Don't be afraid to switch locations a few times a day. It may sound strange, but it makes a world of difference.

- Rearrange your work environment. Move your desk around, change the pictures, place some new items on your desk or workspace to stimulate you.

- Try working in a different place, in a park, a museum, a church, a coffee shop or a train station. How does this change the way you think?

- Take a different route to work in the morning; try walking rather than catching a bus or a train.

THINK IN NEW AREAS

"Here's to the crazy ones. The misfits. The rebels. The trouble-makers. The round pegs in the square hole. The ones who see things differently. They're not fond of rules. And they have no respect for the status quo. You can quote them, disagree with them, glorify or vilify them. About the only thing you can't do is ignore them. Because they change things. They push the human race forward. And while some may see them as the crazy ones, we see genius. Because the people who are crazy enough to think they can change the world, are the ones who do."

Apple Computer Inc.

The idea

Don't limit your innovations to incremental changes of existing products; look ahead and think about what kinds of problems could be solved or needs met by a whole new product or a new way of thinking. There are thousands of examples of incremental change – where companies are making small changes to things and declaring it as innovation. Although it can be viewed as innovation in some respects, these changes are typically not going to change the world.

I believe innovation is a spectrum – at one end doing things for the sake of it to the other end, which is where radical innovation occurs. There are fewer examples of true radical innovation than incremental innovation. Radical product innovations are often agents of creative destruction. They threaten to destroy existing market positions, and yet they often yield vast new market opportunities.

Insistent Innovation	Incremental Innovation	Step Change	Changing Step	Radical Innovation	Disruptive Innovation
Doing 'things' for the sake of doing 'things'	Doing 'things' differently	Doing 'things' very differently	Doing different 'things'	Changing the way 'things' work	Changing what 'things' are
Most companies!	Sony PS3 Console	Fuji 3D Compact Camera	Apple iTunes etc.	Dyson Cyclone Vacuum	Nintendo DS/Wii

Figure 7: Six Degrees of Innovation

One great example of a radical or disruptive innovation is Voice Over Internet Protocol (VoIP) which was originally pioneered by the US Defense Department. The market for traditional voice communication had, since its inception in the late 1880s, a steady evolution with its provision being controlled by regulated service providers, historically controlled by governments.

The development and deployment of VOIP service in the early 21st century disrupted the traditional model of telephony provision and brought in a new way for consumers and businesses to make voice and video calls.

Traditional phone networks use a circuit switching approach – when a call is made, circuits are switched in the telephone exchanges creating a 'logical' connection between the caller and the person being called.

In contrast, VoIP employs a technology called packet switching which the Internet is based on. Within these networks, data is divided into small packets, which are given identifying information and are then transported across the network. At the end of the line, they are reassembled to provide the information to the receiver. Historically, packet switching was rarely used for voice calls because the reassembling of information could seriously deteriorate the quality of the call. However, the quality of VoIP is now arguably on the same level as a regular phone call.

It is estimated that there were more than 120 million active VoIP business users worldwide at the end of 2010 (Point Topic), which is estimated to be worth over $30 billion. Consumer service Skype, which launched in 2005, has over 663 million registered users and had a revenue in excess of $1bn in 2010, taking a 13% share of International voice traffic.

The disruptive nature of this innovation was not only in terms of the technology but has caused a massive rethink into the business and commercial models of traditional telephony service providers; with companies such as Skype and Vonage lowering prices on international calls where traditionally, the major telephony companies made significant profits.

In practice

- Think about the ideas you have. Where do they sit on the Degrees framework. How many do you have on the left hand side and how many on the right?

- Using the VoIP example how could you disrupt your market/life/company? Is there an idea or solution that would radically change the way you work or your offering?

TRY SNOWBALLING

"Many ideas grow better when transplanted into another mind than in the one where they sprung up."

Oliver Wendall Holmes

The idea

One great idea can often lead directly to another, and then this new idea can be built on further. The metaphor of a snowball rolling down the mountain is one that can be used when thinking about this approach. As the snowball rolls down the mountain, it grows, collecting more snow and debris as it goes along. Although the initial idea may be an exceptional one it can often benefit from being built on as it 'rolls' along – gathering new 'debris', that is new characteristics and ideas, on the way.

There are two areas this technique can be used in, when thinking about innovation. Firstly, building on an existing idea and secondly, seeing the idea or solution as a platform for other ideas.

By building on an existing idea you can see many new possibilities – new customers, new markets, even new ideas. By adding something to an idea or solution, you can open up a completely new area ripe for innovation. If the new idea or 'add-on' is not appropriate for the current problem, put it to one side and maybe find a use for it later. By building on your idea, you may be able to think about different markets, different customers and even different countries. Try a different approach by adding one of these new dimensions. Ask yourself:

- How could my idea be different in India, in China or the US?

- How would it serve an elderly customer or a child?

- What new market could it open up if I changed it?

The second area where snowballing can be used is when considering your idea or solution as a platform that others could build on. This is being widely talked about in marketing terms today with companies such as Google. In the case of Google, they provide the platform (the mountain) and allow other businesses that can profit from its platform. The idea of the snowball is that on these smaller platforms, other businesses grow and so it goes on. Maybe these can be considered as the debris that a snowball gathers – not adding extra snow but providing a platform for the debris to find the underlying cause of the mountain!

The snowball continues to grow as it travels down this never-ending slope; all the time Google continues to make money without having to do anything except ensure that the platform is there (the slope is steep enough to maintain the snowball's descent). The platform continues to grow because Google has millions of snowballs hurtling down their virtual mountains all the time, and a constant supply of new ones ready to roll.

In practice

Write your idea at the top of a large sheet of paper. Draw a line down the middle. On the left side of the page write all the ways the idea can be improved. On the right of the page write down all the things that can be 'enabled' by your idea – what else could benefit, what other things could it facilitate. Once you have your two lists, select the best three on each side and try to incorporate them into your original idea.

- Pull together your idea into a 'pitch' you would give to a venture capitalist (such as on the *Dragons' Den* television programme). Think about why they would want to invest in your idea? What is special about your idea? What other opportunities do you think they might see?

- Think about how your idea could 'snowball' into others. Could other businesses be built on yours? Could you still make money if this happened?

32 READ AS MUCH AS YOU CAN

"Reading furnishes the mind only with materials of knowledge. It is thinking that makes what we read ours."

John Locke

The idea

Books, magazines, newspapers, websites, all exercise your brain, provide inspiration, fill you with information, and give you insights which allow you to make innovative connections easily.

The information you absorb provides you with a 'data bank' of possible connections and sources of inspiration. Innovation is all about creating links between disparate elements, business models and information, and to effectively achieve this you need to have input from different areas, topics, viewpoints, industries, etc.

Although not directly related to reading, the story of the first iPod is a great example of serendipity and linking. Apparently, the idea for the iPod came in a bathroom when the designer handled a bar of soap. The touch and feel of the soap triggered an idea for a design for a new music player.

The key to adopting this technique is to be very open about what and where you read. Take the opportunity to read any time you have free time; use it to fill your mind with new information. Not all of it will stick but it will be there in your subconscious for use later on.

When you do read think about the key themes that are apparent to you; it will be these themes that you need to commit to memory as they will provide the links later on. It may be useful to write them down as the act of writing things down has proven to help memory retention.

Gadgets such as the iPad and Kindle provide access to many more books and magazines in a handy form. These devices also allow you to highlight phrases and paragraphs for use later. I use an iPad to read books as it also gives me access to applications such as Excel where I can capture new ideas and insights.

In practice

- Plan to read at least one book per month. It may be a good idea to join a book club, as this will give you a random selection of books to read. However, this can work out to be expensive if you don't read the books.

- Ask friends or colleagues for books to read. Most people have books on their bookshelves that they would be happy to lend you.

- For birthdays and at Christmas, ask people to buy you *their* favourite book – you will be surprised what you get – don't be dismissive, read them because they are all 'fuel' for your innovation engine.

- Look at buying an eBook reader such as a Kindle or iPad, which you can carry around with you. Think about how you can get the most out of these devices, not only for reading, but capturing your ideas.

PRACTICE CREATIVITY

"Creativity is a force moving through us, and only through practice do we learn how to cooperate with it. The 'process' is like a muscle. It needs to be exercised in order to function effortlessly."

Shaun McNiff

The idea

Creativity is very much a skill that you can learn – but like any skill, you need to practice it for at least 30 minutes a day to become proficient. The old maxim 'if you don't use it you lose it' is certainly true for creativity. Creativity is like a muscle, as Shaun McNiff says, the more you use it the stronger it gets, the less you use it the weaker it gets.

Creativity techniques (a shortlist is included in the further reading section at the end of the book) tend to distill down to a few key principles:

- Stimulate – typically through randomness, using an object, a word or a place to provide stimulation for your thoughts.

- Generate – use techniques such as Brainstorming to generate lateral or tangential ideas based on a theme or area. The more you can generate the more likely you are to come up with that great idea – remember the success rate for ideas is around 3% – 7%.

- Un-think – Looking at things differently. Look at a problem, an opportunity or an idea from a different perspective; this can be from a different person's viewpoint, a different industry or sector or any other 'lens' from which you can view things.

There are many permutations of these techniques and the key to using them is to find what works for you.

Try addressing a possible need or a problem with these different techniques and see what outcome you get. You might be surprised to find that output varies depending on the technique and the person using it. It all depends on the individual, their experience, their way of thinking and the environment they are in.

One of the secrets of creativity is to force yourself to do things differently so do try something new and don't just go for the easy option!

Practicing creativity can be a beneficial activity as it is mentally rewarding and can create a feeling of excitement, producing a positive 'aura' around you which can rub off on others.

In practice

- Make a list of creativity techniques, either from this book or from some other source. Then make another list of random topics taken from a newspaper or a magazine. When you have your two lists, pick one word from each list at random and see what ideas you come up with.

- The Internet is a great resource for finding new and interesting creativity tools and techniques so plan to spend time surfing the web.

- When you have a new idea or problem try at least four ways of thinking about it – more if you have time. Look for similarity, look for connections and look for new insights.

- Try using a technique with different people – see if different results ensue.

34 FIGHT YOUR FEAR OF FAILURE

The idea

The fear that you might make a mistake or fail in your efforts can hinder your progress. Whenever you find yourself experiencing fear of failure, remind yourself that mistakes are simply part of the process. Edison famously said that he didn't fail, he just found thousands of ways not to do something.

As with many other fears, the fear of failure or Atychiphobia, is an extreme, irrational fear which can stop you from getting any value from your ideas. The risk is that your fear is so strong that you subconsciously undermine your own efforts – convincing yourself that you don't have to continue, that you haven't got what it takes to succeed. Like so many fears, this phobia is often so strong it becomes a self-fulfilling prophecy, causing the very failure that was feared.

The best way to beat this fear is to face it, accepting that failure is simply necessary for success and realising that you can learn a lot from failing. Recognising the positive value of failure is something that successful innovators relish. Remember there is no failure, only feedback. Successful innovators see mistakes as unintended outcomes or unexpected results, not as failure.

"Whatever humans have learned had to be learned as a consequence only of trial and error experience. Humans have learned only through mistakes."

Richard Buckminster Fuller, Anwar S. Dil (*Humans in Universe*)

The secret of overcoming this fear is to face it and do something that frightens you. If you knew for sure that you couldn't fail, what would you do? Do it NOW!

If you do face challenges or problems don't give up. Successful people find ways around problems – after all this is what innovation is all about.

I think the most important lesson I have learnt from all my years in business is – if you are going to fail, fail fast, learn from it and move on.

In practice

- Look back at things in your life where you didn't do things because you were afraid. Identify exactly what it was that you were afraid of – was it humiliation, peer criticism, financial problems, fear of criticism or something else. On reflection what would have been the outcome if you had gone ahead?

- Choose to do something that you have been too frightened to do in the past; maybe go on a roller coaster, a parachute or bungee jump, or it could be public speaking. Force yourself to do it – it will be uncomfortable and you may decide that you never want to do it again – but you might just find a new passion!

- Make a list of what could stop you from achieving your desired outcome. For each item on the list, write three ways of getting around it.

35 | THINK ABOUT THE ENVIRONMENTAL IMPACT

"All my life I have tried to pluck a thistle and plant a flower wherever the flower would grow in thought and mind."

Abraham Lincoln

The idea

The environment is becoming an important factor for individuals and business alike as climate change becomes a reality. This focus on the environment is providing new opportunities for innovation, in areas as diverse as alternative energy, carbon and water footprinting, recycling, 'green' products and services, as well as many others.

If you have an idea or a solution to a problem, think about the environmental factors that might influence it as well as the opportunities that taking a 'green' approach could bring. If it is a product, think about packaging, distribution, marketing and the technology that is required to support it.

The concept of carbon footprinting (how much carbon dioxide is emitted in the production and operation of a product or service) and more recently water footprinting (how much water is used in the production and operation of a product or service and where it is sourced from) are becoming common words in business.

Both of these look at the impact of the business on the planet, and in particular the impact of the company's products and services on the environment. The carbon impact of a company is being included in annual reports and accounts and is of increasing importance to shareholders and customers. The use of water is something that has only just become a factor as we face unpredictable weather; it is likely to become as important, or even more important than carbon, as its scarcity increases. We will always have plenty of carbon but we won't always have this much water!

I was working with a major global FMCG (fast moving consumer goods) company a few months ago on new products in the ice cream market. There was some research into the product that showed that the huge carbon footprint that ice cream has is primarily in the distribution and storage of the product. The insight from the work was that, if the product could be produced locally then the carbon footprint would be massively reduced. There would also be major cost savings on refrigerated delivery.

Although this started out as a new product initiative, the resultant outcome was incredibly well received by the company and consumers. This simple insight allowed the company to launch a new marketing campaign, increased sales, changed the way the company looked at its products and services, and transformed the consumer perception of this giant corporation.

The environmental impact of your idea or solution could be something that provides an insight, which would give you an edge, an opportunity to address a new market, or customer, as well as providing a good marketing message.

In practice

- Think about how your idea/solution will affect the environment. Take an environmental slant, can you 'green' your idea/solution?

- Look closely at your idea/solution and write down all the 'green' opportunities that could be built on it. Ask yourself:

  - Are there opportunities for reducing the carbon or water footprint?

  - Could it remove something from the production process or allow something to be recycled?

  - Would it reduce an individual's or a company's carbon impact?

- Try reversing the problem – how could it be the most environmentally unfriendly product or service? Did this give you any new insights?

36 UNDERSTAND YOUR BIORHYTHMS

"Action and reaction, ebb and flow, trial and error, change – this is the rhythm of living. Out of our over-confidence, fear; out of our fear, clearer vision, fresh hope. And out of hope, progress."

Bruce Barton

The idea

It may seem strange to include this idea under innovation but it is relevant because of its significance to creativity. We all have our own natural rhythms, times when we are alert and awake, times when we are relaxed, times when we get more stressed, times when we are just out of sorts.

Our biorhythms can vary depending on the amount of daylight, the temperature and even how much sleep we have had.

Most of us are at our creative best after we get up in the morning – termed the 'golden hour.' Many people use this as their creative time, choosing to write, paint or to learn something new at this early hour. Experts recommend this is the best time to read, listen to self-help books and ponder ideas.

However, this is not true for everyone and there is a section of the community that is more productive and inventive after lunch or late into the afternoon. The secret is to understand your own rhythms – find out how your body and mind works.

Although there are some tools on the web that purport to calculate your biorhythms for you using your date and time of birth, they can be misleading; the best and the only way I have found which is accurate is to monitor your own feelings, thoughts and performance.

By finding your 'sweet spot' for creativity, your most productive time of day, you will enhance your ability to generate those amazing ideas.

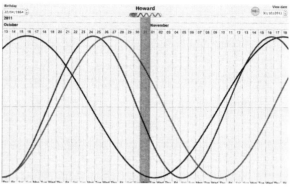

Figure 8: Biorhythms

In practice

- Set yourself the task of generating ideas at different times of the day. Take the same problem and try it first thing in the morning. Wait a couple of days and then try it at 11am. Continue through the day and see if you are better at certain times.

- Note the times of day when you are most creative verbally, visually, kinesthetically, etc., and structure your day to maximise your use of creative energy. Periodically, experiment with modifying your schedule.

- Encourage others around you to go through this exercise so you can work more effectively with them on an ongoing basis.

- Search the Internet for tools that plot your biorhythm; try using the output as a guide for undertaking innovation and creativity exercises. Are the results any different from what you would have expected?

37 ☕ CREATE AN IDEAL COMPETITOR

"The value of innovation is about making the competition irrelevant by creating uncontested market space. We argue that beating the competition within the confines of the existing industry is not the way to create profitable growth."

W. Chan Kim and Renee Mauborgne

The idea

Great innovation often appears when we are faced with adversity, whether it is related to war, natural disasters, illness or something simpler such as competition. The threat factor 'forces' us to think and do things differently, to be creative and innovative.

In 2011, as the global economy struggles with the European debt crisis and other economic issues, budgets are decreasing while staff cuts are growing, making innovation increasingly difficult. However, it is even more important to find new and innovative ways to develop ideas and solutions during difficult financial times. It is exactly in this sort of difficult economic environment that innovation pays off.

There are numerous examples of adversity fostering innovation such as the bouncing bomb developed by Barnes Wallace in the Second World War when there was a need to destroy dam walls. Given the small dam wall and the depth of the water, ordinary bombs were ineffective. Barnes Wallace watched a small boy skimming a stone across a pond and sought to see if this idea could be transferred to developing a bomb that would be positioned against the wall.

"Adversity reveals genius, prosperity conceals it."

Horace (Roman Poet)

Another example of adversity bringing about innovation is the flooding that took place in and around Brisbane, Australia in January, 2011. One company had the idea of creating a website that allowed local businesses to offer goods and services to those affected by the floods, typically at cost. On its launch, the website was swamped with companies keen to offer goods for sale and people who needed them. If the disaster had never happened this site would not have existed and this new way of conducting business would never have emerged. The idea is now being extended to other areas.

To leverage the creative power of adversity, you need to set up a 'threatening' situation that will 'force' you to become more innovative. As an exercise, set up a new competitor, one who will, if unchecked, devastate your revenue and your market share. Make it as real as you can.

Some organisations actually set up a team to act out the board of the competitor and play out their entry into the market. Often a competitor will 'attack' the weak spots of your business by using an internal team with members who know your business inside out. Thus you will be able to quickly identify any areas of weakness or vulnerability.

Reflect on what you have learnt, what insights you got and how you can incorporate these learnings into your current operation?

In practice

Imagine a powerful competitor who can defeat you. Study them, get to know them, make it real, maybe go as far as creating posters, ad campaigns, sales strategies, etc. Then BE them – role-play their actions. Reflect on their strategy, their approach to your customers. What can you learn from this exercise? What insights have you gained?

Build a strategy that will counter the competitors' 'attack' on your business.

Think about a competitor who would not normally be considered; a favourite one at the moment is Google.

- How would Google approach your market or customers?

- How would the company gain market share?

- How would you respond to Google's strategy?

Pick companies off the stock market list at random, and consider how they would approach your idea using their business model or strategy. Don't worry if the company isn't a natural player, it doesn't matter – this is a good exercise in thinking outside the box.

TAKE A BATH

"A conventional good read is usually a bad read, a relaxing bath in what we know already. A true good read is surely an act of innovative creation in which we, the readers, become conspirators."

Augustine Birrell

The idea

In a world filled with a constant call to action, it is important that we stop to think from time to time. Something that seems to be a luxury for many, is a vital part of being innovative.

It may seem strange but, believe it or not, the bathroom is where most people have their best ideas. The combination of solitude, silence and security provide the time and space to think. There is even a Facebook group called 'Thinking in the bathroom"!

"I am usually most creative when I am in the bathroom (taking a shower). There have been so many times in my life I have to write essays, give presentations in front of the public. No matter how much time I spend in the library or in a quiet room, no matter how hard I try, I have not always been satisfied with the ideas I devise. However, 1–2 days before an assignment is due, the panic in me just makes me think about what I will have to say or write, and I usually do that when I take a shower. Ideas just keep popping up in my head, organising themselves and getting ready to go. Most of my crazy creativities come from the bathroom. I thought I was the only one who was weird."

– Martin W., New York University student

Throughout my hectic life I have made it a point to do what many people fail to do on a daily basis, reflect on who I have spoken to, what I have seen or read that day and so on. I do some of my best thinking, not in the office or in my car, but in the bathroom.

The bathroom has always been where I can relax, an oasis of calm and contemplation. The closest thing to an interruption is a polite knock on the door. In short, the bathroom is the ideal place for introspection, critical thought and inspiration. Here I take solace in silence and retreat from the stresses of life.

The bathroom is not a place to escape the challenges of reality, but rather a place to embrace new ideas and conquer challenges.

One element which helps is that many bathrooms have tiled walls and mirrors which make a great whiteboard. Be careful though to only use Dry-Wipe pens and don't get any on the grout in between the tiles!

In practice

- Next time you go to the bathroom take a notepad with you! It might seem strange but before you go in write down your problem or your idea and then take the time to jot down your thoughts.

BRING IN DIVERSITY

The idea

We all believe that everyone thinks like us, has had our experiences and sees the world as we do; the reality is just the opposite. We are all individuals, have had a unique set of experiences, and see the world in a unique way. By bringing diversity into our thinking, we open ourselves up for new insights and challenges.

View the situation as if you know nothing about it. Extend your circle beyond people who think and act just like you. Edison realised "... sameness doesn't serve your evolving mastermind collaboration efforts." What matters is cultivating connections and conversations with people of different generations, industries, cultures, interests and backgrounds. With people who have had diverse experiences.

Globalisation and immigration have driven diversity in many countries; that means that it is highly probable that you will have access to a wide network of people with different thoughts and values to yourself. Use this network to challenge your preconceptions and thoughts. Test your ideas and be open to a new way of thinking. The social media explosion on the Internet also provides an opportunity to engage with a diverse group of people and contacts.

There is research from the US that suggests that businesses with a disparate workforce tend to do better. The research shows that diversity not only brings a range of ideas and information, but it changes the way that everyone thinks and acts. This is also true for individuals. Having a diverse group of friends and colleagues changes how we think – recognise this and exploit it in your innovation activities.

"It is ironic that companies so often pretend to celebrate 'diversity' while systematically stamping it out. The kind of diversity that really counts is ... diversity of thinking."

Gary Hammel

In practice

- Actively seek out diversity in your circle of friends and colleagues – find out other people's views, experiences and insights.

- When on vacation or on a business trip, take time to seek out local people and cultural landmarks – try to view the world from their perspective and understand how history and local conditions shape thinking and values.

- Join social media networks such as LinkedIn or Google Groups and engage in discussions and conversations. Use this resource carefully, especially if discussing your idea or solution.

PART 3

PEOPLE

Inspired, passionate and enthusiastic people, not people who are half-hearted about life, create change.

40 | EXCITE YOUR TEAM

"The organisations of the future will increasingly depend on the creativity of their members to survive. Great groups offer a new model in which the leader is an equal among titans. In a truly creative collaboration, work is pleasure, and the only rules and procedures are those that advance the common cause."

Warren Bennis

The idea

One of the problems with teams, whether this is at work or at home, is that they can get stale over time. In 1965, Bruce Tuckman proposed a model of team development which is still valid today. I have extended it for this book.

Teams typically go through a number of stages; first they 'form' – they come together as a group and people find out about each other.

The next stage is 'storming' – this is the phase where conflict surfaces. People start to posture for position, influence and 'power' within the team. This is the exploratory stage when tensions and conflicts surface. Although this phase can be uncomfortable it is where some of the best ideas surface.

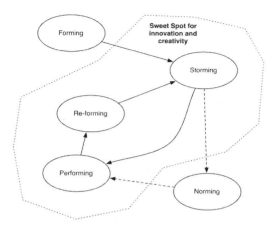

Figure 9: Storming, Forming, Norming, Re-forming

The next stage in the Tuckman model is 'norming' where the team settles down and starts to work effectively as a group. For creative and innovation teams, this can be quite a destructive phase as the group moves towards 'groupthink' where there is acceptance of ideas rather than challenge. If innovation and creativity is important to the team, the restrictions of this phase need to be recognised.

The next phase in the Tuckman model is 'performing' – this is where the team finds its feet, understands where its strengths lie and becomes effective. Although this is where the team provides most value, it is probably where it is less innovative and creative. If you are delivering an idea, this is the most effective phase of the Tuckman model.

I suggest that there is another phase to the model – that of 're-forming'. In this phase, the group restructures – bringing in new people, connecting with other teams and redefining what the team's values and goals are. This then leads back to the 'storming' phase.

These last three phases are where teams are the most creative and innovative, and there can be a palpable sense of excitement within the team. I don't suggest that you encourage conflict within the team though this can be a contributory factor to innovation and creativity.

Some of the benefits of creating excitement in your team are:

- Increase in team morale

- An injection of creativity and the willingness to contribute new ideas

- Focus on delivering the team's goals

- 100% participation and interaction

- Fun, more fun and laughter

In practice

- Try new ways of bringing fun into the team – team building, interesting challenges, charity work.

- One way to challenge the team is to introduce conflict and adversity. Instead of asking, "How can I improve service to customers?" you can ask "How can I make the service so bad that it scares customers away for life?"

- Create a video ad for the team which brings out the personalities of the team members as well as their values and goals.

- Brand the team – this gives them identity and focus.

41 FOSTER ENTHUSIASM – IT'S INFECTIOUS

The idea

Enthusiasm is a great driver for creative and innovative thinking. It inspires others and encourages us to overcome our limitations to find our true potential. We need enthusiasm to keep the spark of innovation and creativity alive. In addition, of course enthusiasm is fun and infectious!

There are few things more enjoyable than talking enthusiastically about something you are passionate about, particularly where you can inspire others and engage them in your vision. The excitement of not knowing what you're going to say next causes uncertainty and surprise. It also makes the vision more meaningful to the people you are talking to.

When you talk enthusiastically, you create stories with images, ideas and words in other people's minds. You find ways of encouraging people to 'buy in' to your ideas or solutions. Lead by example. You have to be enthusiastic yourself to foster enthusiasm in others.

Think back to a time when you heard someone talk enthusiastically about a topic or idea that was of little interest to you. Didn't you feel that you could not help being fascinated, intrigued by what they were saying and wanted to know more? There is something contagious about the body language of someone with enthusiasm –

their gestures, their facial expression, the tone of their voice, their energy – you just can't help responding. You can't resist the urge to join in, to be part of whatever it is they are talking about.

Enthusiasm can overcome many setbacks we face when we try to convince people about our ideas or solutions. If we are not determined and enthusiastic, we have a tendency to give up. With enthusiasm success can be created and obstacles overcome, in even the most difficult circumstances.

There is an old Jewish proverb that says drive your horse with oats, not with a whip. Give yourself a goal to work towards, particularly when working within a team. Instead of having them work to avoid punishment, give them something to strive towards.

If we want to create something memorable, we need to be inspirational in our communication with others. It is unlikely that you will be able to deliver your great idea by yourself – you will need other people around you to help you. It is no good having a vision if you keep it to yourself. It is your enthusiasm, your dynamism, your energy and passion which will encourage others to join your crusade. If you are indifferent, you will immediately turn people off.

Change is created by inspired and enthusiastic people, not by people who are half-hearted about life.

Don't forget, just like laughter, enthusiasm is contagious so spread it.

In practice

- Change your behaviour, plan to be enthusiastic. Become that positive person you always wanted to be!

- Try communicating an idea in a very matter-of-fact way, and then try the same thing with enthusiasm. Watch what happens to your audience? Is the response different?

- Look for enthusiastic people to talk to. What effect do they have on you, how do you feel about what they are telling you?

- Complaining can be contagious. Don't allow it to occur around you. Turn negatives into positives. Actively suppress any negativity in your initiative.

42 ASK SOMEONE NEW FOR COFFEE

"In everyone's life, at some time, our inner fire goes out. It is then burst into flame by an encounter with another human being. We should all be thankful for those people who rekindle the inner spirit."

Albert Schweitzer

The idea

So often we are trapped in our comfort zone, we go to the same place for lunch, meet the same people, do the same things. Although this is the 'easy' way, and there is security in the familiar, it does not stimulate our minds and bring us experiences that we can use to gain new insights. An approach which can help you get out of this 'zone' is to actively plan to meet new people, find new places, find stimulation for your ideas.

By actively seeking out new people, we open ourselves up to acquire new ideas and create potential sources of support to achieve our goals. Someone new may also introduce us to new environments, new tastes and new friends, all of which could help stimulate new ideas.

There are two elements to this idea – one is the environment of a coffee shop itself and the community it creates – the second is the people you associate with.

Let us first look at the environment of the coffee shop. In his book, *Tribes,* Seth Godin talks about how communities form around shared values and interests. As a frequent visitor to a local coffee shop myself, most of this book was written in one, I can understand Seth's viewpoint as I feel completely at home and at my most productive there.

It is not at all uncommon for me to start a conversation with a stranger at a coffee shop, or for a stranger to start a conversation with me. Coffee shops offer a social opportunity for networking and making new friends. I have been amazed at the number of new people I have met and the conversation I have had at these places. A few of these conversations have led on to ideas for books, highly productive connections with companies and new insights into other people's worlds.

The second element is the people you choose to associate with. While in an office or family environment this can be hard to change, as there may be peer pressure to 'conform', by actively seeking out new people for a coffee, you are increasing your social circle and in a work context, this 'network' can be an amazingly useful tool in getting things done.

Therefore, the simple act of asking someone new out for coffee can affect your innovation ability, and along with it maybe even your career.

In practice

- Set yourself a target of asking someone new out for coffee every week.

- Actively seek out new coffee shops and plan to visit one every month.

- Start a conversation with a stranger at least once a week. Try and find common ground, maybe even float your latest idea and see what transpires.

43 COMMUNICATE, COMMUNICATE, COMMUNICATE

"In the modern world of business it is useless to be a creative original thinker unless you can also sell what you create. Management cannot be expected to recognise a good idea unless it is presented to them by a good salesperson."

David M. Ogilvy

The idea

Communication is the lifeblood of innovation. Over the last 15 years of working in the field of innovation and creativity, I have found that one of the keys to success is good communication. This works at many levels; at the most basic, you communicate your idea to others with your passion and enthusiasm, as well as your clarity of vision on what you are trying to achieve.

At another level your communication creates a 'buzz', it gets people talking, not only about what you are doing but also about you as an individual. This becomes increasingly important as you look for supporters and sponsors for your ideas. Social media sites such as LinkedIn and Facebook can be great places to foster this buzz. Blogging can also be used effectively to create a community around you and your ideas. An innovative idea has a way of going viral on these social media sites – the key is to get the timing right for lighting the 'fire'.

Communication is also vital in getting a 'buy-in' for your ideas. Gaining a coalition of supporters and advocates early on is an essential element of success, especially in large organisations.

Innovation is not something that you can do alone. Although you need to be the one with the vision and the passion, you need to have people around to support your endeavours and to provide you with new connections and insights. Chances are that you won't have all the skills, knowledge and contacts that you will require to achieve your goal. Finding people who have these skills will be a key factor in the success of your initiative.

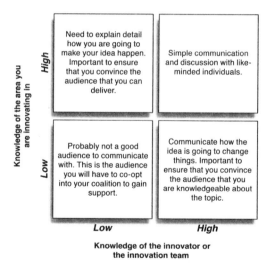

Figure 10: Communication Matrix

By communicating our ideas we give others permission to have their own ideas. A noteworthy example of this is when I was working with a large UK government department running a series of innovation workshops. Only a few staff members attended the workshops, which were aimed at incremental improvements to the day-to-day processes within their offices. The attendees, who got excited about the activities, went back to their offices fired up and full of enthusiasm. This enthusiasm rubbed off on their colleagues who hadn't attended the workshop but caught the innovation bug and made some valuable contributions to the project.

To be effective it is important to make sure you have given sufficient thought to the messages you want to get across. In other words, you need to develop a communication strategy early on in your initiative and tailor your communications to the audience you are addressing.

In practice

- Tell people about the exciting ideas you have, or the solutions you have found.

- Set up a blog on the things you are doing. Invite people to comment and add to your ideas/solutions.

- Build your elevator pitch – your 90-second sales pitch for your idea. An elevator pitch is used to quickly define a product, service or idea and the potential value it could bring. The term originated in Hollywood when aspiring actors planned to take the elevator with a producer and used the time between floors to sell their concept to him.

- Develop a communications strategy that not only looks at communicating your idea, but also how you communicate with your team and supporters.

- Think about the consequential effect of your communication. Who else could it impact and what might the effect be?

BECOME AN EVANGELIST FOR INNOVATION

"Passion is the seed of innovation."

Sanjay Dalal

"... evangelist is not a title, it's a way of life."

Guy Kawasaki

The idea

Passion about what you are doing will not only make or break your innovation activities, it will create an environment of change, an excitement in those around you. Innovation is something that many people aspire to but few do anything about because they don't understand what it is and what being innovative actually means.

By becoming an evangelist you give focus and direction to people, you provide a framework for them to work within and move their ideas forward. As there are so many different views of what innovation is, and what defines success, it is important to have clarity on what innovation means to you and how it differs from creativity.

Being an innovation evangelist is not an easy job, either within an organisation or outside it. Guy Kawasaki says, "Evangelist is not a title, it's a way of life." An innovation evangelist is someone who seeks to convert a minority (lead adopters) about a concept, to the majority (the mainstream).

Unfortunately, most organisations squash passion. This is why start-ups have a much easier time innovating than FTSE 100 companies.

Moreover, this is why perceptive FTSE 100 companies recreate the feeling of a start-up whenever they can through spin-out activities. If you look at any large organisation, less than 3% of the employees can be considered innovative. These individuals are often ignored and sidelined, as they don't fit in with the normal company profile.

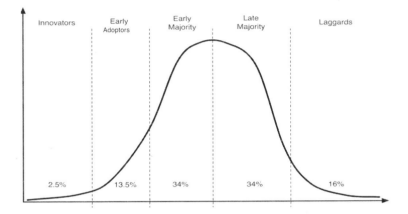

Figure 11: Company Innovation Profile

One of the things I have learnt over the years I have worked in innovation is that external recognition is worth more than internal recognition. Why is this important?

If you become an innovation evangelist purely within an organisation, you will face adversity on a daily basis as you will be pushing against the 'status quo,' against the pervasive culture within the company. By gaining external recognition, you make it easier for the organisation to accept you as an individual, and accept you for what you stand for.

In practice

- Become an evangelist for what you are doing and recruit others to your cause of innovation.

- Define what YOU mean by innovation and what model or framework you subscribe to.

- Define what success would mean to you, both in business and personal terms.

- Prepare an elevator pitch and use it to explain what you are doing. By creating the pitch, you make it easier for people to tell your story. Attend networking events and use them to promote your ideas.

45 WHO ARE YOU INNOVATING FOR?

"Yearn to understand first and to be understood second."

Beca Lewis

The idea

There is no single answer to this question as everyone has a different story to tell about how they got to where they are. Some started with an idea or a solution, a vision of how things could be different while others began with the challenge of coming up with a goal or an objective. The reality is that most people are somewhere in the middle.

Understanding why you are innovating, or why you want to innovate, whether you are doing it for your company or yourself, are key questions that can shape your behaviour and the outcomes you are seeking.

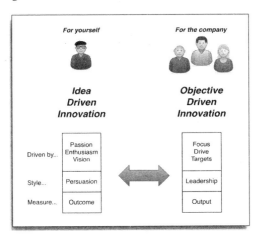

Figure 12: Why are you Innovating?

Another question to ask yourself is: are you enamoured with the idea of being an innovator or do you have a real passion for it? Is it a job, a career or a way of life?

Next you need to consider the drivers of the innovation activity. In Figure 12, I have tried to identify how the drivers and measures are different if you are innovating for yourself versus innovating for your company. As you can see, if you are company focused, innovation is more output- and activity-focused, driven by targets and deriving value.

If the innovation is driven by an idea you have, then the drivers are more personal such as passion, enthusiasm and the vision you have for whatever it is that you want to achieve.

I hope that you can see from this model that if you are trying to initiate an idea-driven innovation in your company, it can prove difficult given that the company is looking for focus, targets and leadership while you are bringing in passion, enthusiasm and vision.

Many people get involved in innovation thinking they are doing it for the company when in reality they are doing it for themselves. This can lead to a stressful situation since personal objectives and goals are not aligned to company objectives and targets which usually ends in frustration and failure.

Understanding why you are doing something will provide self-awareness that should enable you to adopt the right attitude and style of working.

Although the model looks at the situation from a 'binary' perspective – either one or the other – the reality is that this is a spectrum and there are many gradations in between. Focus on thinking about your own needs from the project and then, if you are innovating in a company, think about its needs.

In practice

- Who will benefit most from what you are doing and why?

- What would success look like and what will be different if you are successful?

- How important are your personal goals?

46 ATTEND CONFERENCES THAT ARE 'OFF-TOPIC'

"In a person who is open to experience, each stimulus is freely relayed through the nervous system, without being distorted by any process of defensiveness."

Carl Rogers

The idea

Finding alternative stimulus can be extremely beneficial. Not only do you get a different point of view, new insights and ideas, but also the opportunity to meet interesting people which can be truly life changing.

Although this chapter is titled conferences, what I mean is gatherings of people where there will be discussion and information that you wouldn't normally be exposed to. This could be a local business networking meeting, a political meeting, a pressure group and anything else that will provide you with a different view.

One of the best 'off topic' conferences I have attended is TED (www. TED.com) in the US where 3,000 – 4,000 people from extremely diverse backgrounds get together specifically to hear different viewpoints and discuss. I remember one conference where I was having dinner with a theoretical physicist, a pharmaceutical researcher, a dance teacher, an actor, a 'dot-com' millionaire, a lawyer and a teacher from a local school. Although we all had divergent viewpoints, it was amazing how the conversation flowed, and I left that meal with two great ideas.

By forcing yourself to go to places that may be outside your comfort zone, you not only find out new things and people, but also challenge some of your preconceptions, or maybe reinforce old ones!

In practice

- Plan to visit at least three to four conferences or meetings a year that are off-topic for you and that you wouldn't normally attend.

- Try to find the most obscure meeting you can and make a point of attending it – you may be surprised at the outcome.

- At meetings and conferences don't just listen to the speaker but actively listen to other conversations. I am not saying join in as this could be intrusive, but you may just overhear something that will spark a new idea.

- Set yourself a target of talking to a certain number of people at the next meeting or conference you attend and keep your elevator pitch ready.

47 FOLLOW INTERESTING BLOGGERS AND TWITTERERS

"It's easy to come up with new ideas; the hard part is letting go of what worked for you two years ago, but will soon be out of date."

Roger von Oech

The idea

Blogging on the Internet has given voice to millions of people around the world, with over 152 million blogs (as tracked by BlogPulse) providing insights, opinions and experiences on almost any topic you can think of, from knitting to knotting, car maintenance to rocket science and business topics such as leadership, strategy, marketing, creativity and innovation.

It may take you some time to find blogs you like but persevere and you will eventually find a kindred spirit, someone whose thinking resonates with yours. Once you have found your kindred spirit, look for blogs that have divergent viewpoints, that contradict your way of thinking and your values. These are the sites that will make you think, and possibly provide some inspiration.

Once you have found your blogs, make an effort to contribute to them by asking questions, sharing your thoughts and asking for advice or ideas. The more you contribute, the better you will understand their perspective. You may be surprised to find how helpful and supportive people can be.

I have lost count of the amazingly talented, smart and insightful people I have had an opportunity to interact with on Twitter. Some of these interactions have led to new ideas, others have led to temporary or even more permanent collaborations.

You have an opportunity to consider your personal branding as you engage with the social media space. How you want to be viewed in this new online world could be vital to the success or failure of your interaction.

My experience is that some of the world's leading thinkers and experts are happy to pass on their thoughts, either through their blogs or in their tweets, so give it a try, what have you got to lose?

In practice

- Find bloggers who interest you and follow them on a regular basis.

- Spend some time searching the 'blogosphere' using a website such as www.blogsearchengine.com. When you have found your blogs, sign up for their newsletters and updates.

- Use software to 'mine' the twitter-sphere to find people who are tweeting about subjects you are interested in. You can use tools such as Twitscoop to look at the trends that are being discussed on Twitter, or Tweetdeck to provide an overview of all your social media contacts.

- Choose a random blog or tweet and see how the ideas or statements could be used to help your idea. It may be difficult to find a link at first but persevere and you may be surprised at the insights you get.

48. THINK LIKE A VENTURE CAPITALIST

"You have all the reason in the world to achieve your grandest dreams. Imagination plus innovation equals realisation."

Dennis Waitley

The idea

When embarking on an innovation initiative, it is easy to get embroiled in the project or idea and forget the reality of business. You get caught up in the minutiae or the fine points – how will it be built, the delivery, finance, and who will buy it. Although these are all valid questions and ones that you need to think about if you are going to deliver your idea/solution, there is benefit in standing back and viewing the idea/project from a different standpoint, that of a venture capitalist, someone who is going to invest his or her money in the idea.

The television show *Dragons' Den* is a great place to get you started. Watch the programme a few times and try to understand how the 'dragons' think. Ask yourself questions such as: What are they looking for and why? Is it purely a return on their money or is there something more to it than that? How important is the person presenting the idea?

The first element is to imagine that you are presenting your idea to the dragons – how would you do it, what approach would you take, what would be your sales pitch? Don't worry if your idea is not a product one, but instead a solution to a problem. Nevertheless, plan to present it as an idea for them to invest in. One approach is to get your friends and family to role-play the dragons, so that you can experience what it would be like to present to them.

The second element of this idea is to put yourself in the shoes of one of the dragons; choose the one that is most like you and then think about how you/they would view your idea/solution. Consider questions like what they would say, would they be supportive or would they dismiss you.

Venture capitalists typically are interested in the individual first and then the investment potential. They know that for any idea to be successful the person making it happen has to be credible and has to have the vision and passion to make it happen. If they believe that they will make money from your business, they will invest in it. If they cannot see the potential, you will be rejected. Your goal should be to make them see the potential.

By viewing your idea or solution from the viewpoint of a potential investor, you are providing yourself with a new viewpoint, a new angle. Is this something you would be prepared to invest your hard-earned cash in?

In practice

- Force yourself to think like a venture capitalist, role-play the *Dragons' Den* television show. Consider how the venture capitalist would react to your proposal?

- Build a presentation as if you were going to deliver it on the TV show. Keep it short and snappy and ask your family, friends, or if you are brave enough, your colleagues, to role-play the dragons.

49 LEARN TO LISTEN

"The opposite of talking isn't listening. The opposite of talking is waiting."

Fran Lebowitz

The idea

We tend to stop listening as we get older. We like the sound of our own voice and we are keen to give people the value of our experience. Although this can be positive, at times it can be inappropriate, as we tend to judge what we think is being said rather than listen fully and understand the reality.

I have found men are worse than women when it comes to listening. Men tend to come up with a solution rather than listen carefully and understand. In the book *Why Women Don't Read Maps and Men Don't Listen* by Allan and Barbara Pease, it is suggested that men only listen with half their brain, while women use both sides.

Listening is one of the greatest skills we can have when it comes to innovation. By listening we gain insights, find problems and needs as well as create opportunities to find new ideas.

Listening gives us the time and space to distill what is being said and to think about our response rather than 'knee jerking' with our first impression or thought. The time we take listening to others is not only precious for us but also for those speaking, as it shows our interest and empathy in their story or position.

I was once given a piece of advice that has stuck with me – "you have one mouth but two ears; use them in this proportion and you will become a wiser man." I have found that once you start actively listening, it becomes a habit and you might just enjoy it.

In practice

- Try actively listening for a change. Talk to someone about your idea and then shut up and listen – it will be hard, especially if you are a man, but force yourself to listen and you might be surprised at what you find out.

- The next time you talk to a colleague or one of your friends or family, listen carefully to what they are saying. Take an interest in their story (and try not to look bored)!

- Set yourself a goal of not saying anything in a conversation until 20 seconds after the other person has stopped speaking.

BREAK YOUR ROUTINES

"You can't do today's job with yesterday's methods and still be in business tomorrow."

Anonymous

The idea

Routines can serve a useful purpose; they provide a sense of familiarity and security. However, routines can lead to automation and boredom. It's easy to fall into your comfort zone when you are surrounded by the familiar and the predictable.

Routines can also close the door on innovation and creativity by restricting our thinking. We tend to do the same things day after day, such as getting up at the same time, eating the same breakfast, wearing the same clothing combinations, taking the same route to work, eating lunch at the same places and with the same people. Although all this seems safe, it limits stimulation and provides few opportunities for insights and new ideas.

What are you missing by following the same routine every day?

Small changes in your routine can lead to fresh, invigorating experiences and new thought patterns. It may be that you choose to go to work by a different route each day or use a different mode of transport, a bus or a bicycle instead of a car. Anything that breaks your routine can be a stimulus for new ideas, new perspectives and insights.

I was due for a meeting in London a few weeks ago and rather than take the Underground railway, I decided to walk. While I was walking down one of the side streets I came across a shop selling a brand of shoe that had an RV (camper-van) as its logo. The meeting I was headed to was about a marketing idea for a product. I decided to trash the idea I had prepared and put forward the concept of using an RV to show the product being used on a beach in various locations around the world.

This idea was taken up and used in a series of TV advertisements as well as a prize draw for the RV at the end of the photo shoot. If I had stuck to my routine and used the Underground, I would never have seen the RV/camper-van logo and I may not have got the contract.

By stepping outside my routine, I created an opportunity for new stimulus, new experiences and as it turned out, a new insight. I now force myself to ditch any routine I get into – the secret is recognising when you are in one!

Signs of getting into a rut:

- Your eating, exercise and work routines are set in stone. Do you always take the same train, eat the same cereal for breakfast and the same salad for lunch? Do you experience deja vu when you talk to the same handful of friends about the same things every week?

- Your weekends are starting to blur together. You cannot remember what you did last weekend, as it was the same as all the rest.

- You cannot remember what you did yesterday; days blur into one another.

So, surprise yourself by doing something different. Try changing one thing every day or every week. Monitor the effect this change has on you, and if it was positive do more of it. If not, try something different.

In practice

- Instead of driving to work, take the bus or bicycle, or drive a different route to work each day for a month.

- Go out to lunch with different people at different restaurants.

- Try a new hairstyle or clothing combination. You may get people to notice and pay you compliments – an effective way to start your networking.

- Write a list of things you might like to do, see, or achieve. Can you do any of them in a day? If you are really stuck for ideas, try rolling a dice or flipping a coin. It doesn't really matter what you do, what is important is that you do something different!

CHANGE YOUR ATTITUDE

"He who would be a man must therefore be a non-conformist."

Ralph Waldo Emerson

The idea

Often our attitude to life and work is what holds us back from being innovative and having ideas. We are conditioned from our childhood to conform to social and cultural norms and taught that 'this is the way' things are done. This is reinforced in our early years in the workplace.

As we rise higher in an organisation, the pressure to conform increases and our attitude becomes less individual and more aligned with the organisation. This is particularly true when we progress through promotion boards and performance appraisals.

At home, things are similar and we are taught what is 'right and wrong' from an early age; typically, that conformity is the way forward and that we shouldn't ask why. Interestingly, in much of the Western world, children under five years are encouraged to ask the 'why' question. But as children get older, this behaviour becomes less acceptable.

For innovators, it is a change in attitude that allows them to challenge the status quo and to question the norm. However, many large organisations find it hard to tolerate an innovation function for more than 14 months before its disruptive nature begins to set in. This is the reason why these companies look for innovation and inspiration externally, with consultancies like What-if.

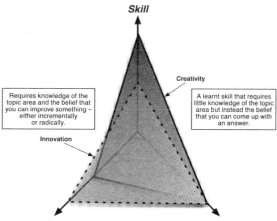

Figure 13: ASK Framework

In the first chapter of this book, I introduced the diagram above that highlights the importance of attitude, both for innovation and for creativity. It is this change in attitude that allows people to look at things differently and to challenge how things have always been done. The model looks at creativity and innovation – creativity in my definition is a learned skill that requires little or no knowledge of the subject in hand. In contrast, innovation is a learned behaviour that uses the knowledge that you already have about a subject and views it from a different perspective. The linkage between these two capabilities is a change in attitude in both cases – an attitude of 'can-do', challenge and curiosity.

In practice

- Change your basic attitude towards your work – re-think your approach to the mundane and repetitive and look for interest in everything you do.

- Look for the positive in any situation. Rather than ask 'why not', think 'what if' and build on other people's ideas.

52 MAKE A LIST – OWN YOUR LIFE

"Decide what you want, decide what you are willing to exchange for it. Establish your priorities and go to work."

H. L. Hunt

The idea

Our lives today are cluttered with all the tasks we have to do, as well as all the things we feel obliged to do for everyone else, that we are unable to just stop and think.

It helps me to write down what I have to do and categorise eveything into one of three areas according to the model on the right.

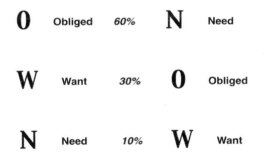

O	Obliged	*60%*	**N**	Need
W	Want	*30%*	**O**	Obliged
N	Need	*10%*	**W**	Want

Obliged is what you have to do at work or at home. There is no question about this, it is how you earn a living or maintain your family/household.

Want is what you dream of. These are the things that you really want to do with your life – the places you want to visit, the things that you want to master and the relationships you want to have.

Need are the things other people make you do – either through guilt, peer pressure or just plain bullying. These are the things that divert you from doing what you are obliged to do or, more importantly, want to do.

Figure 14: NOW to OWN

Much of what I have on the list falls in the 'N' category – things that I need to do, mainly for other people.

The 'O' category is the things that I am obliged to do every day either for work or at home.

The 'W' category has what I want to do and is usually the smallest category on the list. It often gets relegated to the trash can as I usually don't have the time for this category.

When I first did this exercise, I found that I was dedicating less than 10% of my time to things I wanted to do; the majority of what I was doing was what other people were 'making' me do, what I felt I needed to do. Once I realised this, I took positive action to rebalance my life and now I dedicate 30% of my time to things that I want to do, while the need category has been relegated to less than 10% of my time.

The secret to rebalancing my life was to re-prioritise the tasks on my list so that I minimised the need category, which made space for what I wanted to do. This technique also works well for my innovation activities as it helps me re-focus on a daily basis, giving me time to do what I want to do and to have space and time to think.

In practice

- Make a record of your daily tasks for a period of one week and assign an 'O', 'W' or 'N' to each task. At the end of the week, add up the various categories and see if your balance is the same as mine was.

- Get in the habit of making a list every morning, of all the things you have to do that day. Assign each item on the list an 'O' 'W' or 'N'. Then re-order your list from NOW to OWN.

- If you are not able to achieve a task on a particular day, instead of adding it to your next day's list, knock it off your list to avoid stress and anxiety.

ROLE-PLAY

"The winner is the chef who takes the same ingredients as everyone else and produces the best result."

Edward de Bono

The idea

In our working and personal lives, we tend to act according to what we learned from our parents, and during our formative years at school and at college.

This propensity to 'role-play' is apparent the higher people go in an organisation. Few people are natural leaders, and instead they adopt the mannerisms and language of their role models. Over time this behaviour becomes embedded and natural and works extremely well. Other times it can go disastrously wrong with the internal conflict between the natural and the adopted behaviours coming to the fore.

One of the interesting aspects of this role-play is that by acting differently and adopting new behaviours, it is possible to gain new insights and ideas that were lacking previously.

Identify a business leader or manager who has characteristics you admire or aspire to. What is it that makes this person stand out from the crowd? Once you have identified these characteristics or qualities, try being that person for an hour. It can seem strange to those around you so either warn them or lock yourself in a room and think the way they would; adopt their demeanour, their language. Be them!

In practice

- Next time you attend a conference or a business meeting, watch how people conduct themselves. How do they handle particular situations, how do they respond and act?

  - What do you think makes them successful at what they do – try to identify their winning characteristics. Use this insight to role-play your idea or solution, looking at it from a different viewpoint, adopting a different attitude.

- When assessing your idea, role-play a board of directors, look at the idea from a financial director's point of view, a marketing director's, an operational director's and so on. In this role-play, adopt a stance that you think the directors would take, ask questions they would ask, consider what their body language would be, etc. After each role-play, write down any new insights you have had as well as any pertinent questions/points that you need answers to.

- Try taking on a completely different persona for an hour or so; be your favourite actor or TV personality. How would they conduct themselves? What can you learn from this exercise?

BELIEVE IN YOURSELF

"The uncreative mind can spot wrong answers, but it takes a very creative mind to spot wrong questions."

Anthony Jay

The idea

Believe in yourself and your own abilities.

Although this might seem simple, it is easier said than done. Lack of belief in oneself has prevented many people from fulfilling their dreams and achieving great things in their lives. This is particularly true when it comes to promoting a new idea or solution.

We can come up with many excuses to avoid doing something new:

- I am too old.

- I don't know enough to make it happen.

- I won't be able to handle it.

- I don't have the funds for it.

- It will take too much of my time.

- Dealing with all the details will be too time-consuming.

- I am not sure anybody would be interested.

- The economy is too unpredictable.

Innovation is all about having the confidence to take an idea or solution and do something with it. There are thousands of examples of ideas that have fallen by the wayside because people did not believe in themselves and their ability. Very often, the only thing holding you back is you yourself.

Believing in yourself might be a struggle at first, but it gets easier with time. You need to build on small successes which will reinforce your self-belief and change your mindset.

Be someone who thinks about the possibilities rather than the problems. If you train yourself to think big, big things will begin to happen to you.

The secret is to gain a mindset that you can achieve anything you set your mind on. If you look at today's entrepreneurs and business leaders such as Richard Branson and Alan Sugar, you will notice that they have an unerring belief in their abilities. They are no different from you and me. They just achieved this belief in themselves early in their lives; and they spotted an opportunity and did something about it. Were they the best qualified? If you ask them they will probably say no – but they believed in themselves and as far as they were concerned at the time, they couldn't fail.

There is a counter-argument to this unerring self-belief; there needs to be a balance so that you don't become arrogant. You see this balance in Richard Branson, who is humble while exuding a subtle confidence.

In practice

- The next time you come up with an idea, ask yourself: "If you absolutely couldn't fail what would you do?" "What would you do first and then what?" Once you have the first few steps defined, try them and see what happens.

- Set yourself goals. Decide what you want to achieve, write it down and then think about how you are going to achieve it.

- Maintain a positive attitude. Become a champion of the 'why not' club, replace 'but' with 'and' in your daily conversations.

55 GET RID OF SELF-LIMITING HABITS

"Creativity can solve almost any problem. The creative act, the defeat of habit by originality, overcomes everything."

George Lois

The idea

We begin to form habits in our early childhood and combined they make up who we are – our demeanour, our body language, our attitude and our way of thinking. By continually repeating these habits and by living with them, we keep ourselves constrained physically, mentally and emotionally. What we need to do is acquire new habits, but to do so, we first need to break the old ones.

For the purpose of this book, I have split the habits into physical and mental. Physical habits deal with mannerisms like touching your nose when you are not sure about something, repeating a certain phrase, or using a particular facial expression. These are the most obvious habits and typically are the easiest to rectify, once you have recognised them.

The more difficult habits to change are the mental ones; the way you think, the values you have and the beliefs you hold. These habits are not always easy to recognise and you will probably need some outside intervention to help you identify them. It is always more difficult to spot these habits as they are deeply embedded and appear normal to you – 'it's just how I think.'

Whichever habit you want to change, the rule should be 'keep it simple'. Aim to change one or two things at a time, not a hundred. Be very clear about what it is you want to change; one of the best ways to achieve clarity is to write it down.

Simplicity creates habits, complexity creates headaches.

In practice

- Start to document the habits you have. Ask others if they have spotted any habits that you have (this can be a little uncomfortable but go with it, you may get an insight that could change your life)!

- The next time you are in a meeting try to record it (ask permission of course and make it clear that the recording is for your personal use). You may find that you use a particular phrase repeatedly.

- Focus on one change for 30 days since after that time it has been sufficiently conditioned to become a new habit. By adopting this approach, you sculpt the automatic programmes that run in the background of your mind and cause new behaviours and ways of thinking.

56 CREATE THE RIGHT ENVIRONMENT

"Innovation is fostered by information gathered from new connections; from insights gained by journeys into other disciplines or places; from active, collegial networks and fluid, open boundaries. Innovation arises from ongoing circles of exchange, where information is not just accumulated or stored, but created. Knowledge is generated anew from connections that weren't there before."

Margaret J. Wheatley

The idea

Our environment can restrict our thinking and our behavior because we become conditioned to react in a certain way. These conditioned associations are built up over many years and in themselves become habits.

Although these 'habits' are acceptable and allow us to function in our day-to-day life, when we want to think differently they can be limiting, forcing us to maintain the status quo.

An example I use is if you put a chef into a kitchen he is going to do what he has always done. If you put him in a very different environment such as a jungle, a factory, etc., he will probably produce very different food, taking cues and inspiration from what is around him. It's the same with anyone else; we take visual, aural and emotional cues from our surroundings, which affect our thought processes.

While I was working for Royal Mail, I got the opportunity to investigate how the environment conditioned thinking. We undertook a series of idea generation workshops in a variety of places, from churches to hotels, even boats. The results were interesting – when we used conventional spaces such as hotel meeting rooms and conference rooms, the ideas were conservative, when we did the same exercise in unfamiliar spots, the ideas were more 'off the wall'.

As with any habit, the secret is to first recognise it and then look for ways to create a new habit. By visiting new and interesting places, we can stimulate our thoughts and make new connections, gain new insights and have some unique ideas.

In practice

- Plan to visit at least two new places where you can think every month.

- Brainstorm the same idea in different locations – a station, a museum, a cafe, a park or garden and at home – and see if you get different perspectives. Does a pattern emerge; do you find you are taking cues from these different places?

- Use toys and humour to loosen people up and put them in a playful mood. The more relaxed people are, the easier it is for them to envision new possibilities and be open to new ideas.

57 UNDERSTAND THE PROBLEM

"If you're not prepared to be wrong, you'll never come up with anything original."

Sir Ken Robinson

The idea

The secret behind many notable innovations is the innovator's ability to understand the fundamentals of the issue/need/problem that is being addressed.

Often people come up with ideas that on the surface are exceptional, but they don't address the real need or problem. We assume that we understand the situation, but in reality, we are looking at it from our own perspective.

When we get involved with an idea or a solution it is easy to convince ourselves of its validity otherwise we wouldn't have the enthusiasm and passion to turn it into a reality.

You only have to watch a couple of episodes of *Dragons' Den* on television to realise that many ideas are just not viable or suitable. Unless there is a customer for the idea, it has little actual value.

So how do you get to the core of the need or problem? I have included a list of questions to help you understand more fully the need or problem you are trying to address in the model.

Need or problem statement (no more than 50 words):

Who has the need/problem?

Who will benefit from the solution?

What is different about your idea/solution?

What needs to be in place for this great idea/solution to happen?

How else could the need/problem be served?

Figure 15: Problem Analysis Framework

The first thing to do is to write it down as a simple one-line statement which is easy to understand. Test it out with family and friends and see if they recognise it.

Next write down who has the need or problem, be realistic here as this will provide an idea of scale when it comes to assessing the market and benefit. Then ask yourself who is going to benefit from the idea/solution, and why your idea is different. What is it about your idea that is different from what is already in place? This is the time to do some Internet searching, particularly patent databases.

The next question focuses on what needs to be in place for the idea/solution to be workable. Very often noteworthy ideas are thwarted because some critical element is not in place or some environmental factor is missing. Write down if these are in your control or not – can you influence them?

The last questions I suggest are: How else could the need/problem be serviced? Is there another solution? This should focus your thinking on other ways of meeting the need.

In practice

- Complete the framework in Figure 15 for your idea/solution. Be realistic in your responses!

- Talk your idea/solution out with as many people as you can to validate it.

- Research on the Internet. Don't just rely on search engines such as Google but use search aggregators like Dogpile to widen your search. Check out patent databases around the world to see if your idea has already been implemented elsewhere.

SET UP AN IDEAS WALL

"Ideas are the beginning points of all fortunes."

Napoleon Hill

The idea

Make your ideas visible. Set up a space at home or in your workplace where you can post your ideas so they are visible every time you walk in.

By making them visible they become part of your everyday life and are constantly with you. This visibility allows your subconscious mind to continue to work on them in the background.

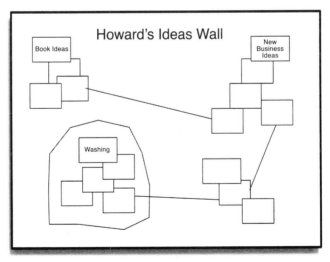

Figure 16: Ideas Wall Example

You will be surprised when ideas pop in to your mind, and remember to capture them as you go through your day. Keep a notebook with you to record your ideas, and post them on your ideas wall.

Once you have a few ideas on your wall, look for connections, commonality and clusters. Is there a common theme, are there links between the ideas?

Keep your wall alive – revisit it every morning before you go to work. This way, you programme your subconscious to work on your ideas during the day. At the end of the day, visit your wall again and you may discover new linkages and solutions.

In practice

- Set up an ideas wall at home and maybe in the office too. Use an old notice board or buy a piece of plywood from your local DIY store.

- Keep a good supply of post-it notes available to record your ideas.

- Keep your wall alive, visit it at least twice a day.

- Try mind mapping software on your laptop, iPad or phone. Map your ideas and look for linkages and groupings.

SET UP AN IDEAS BANK

"Luck is what happens when preparation meets opportunity."

Seneca (Roman Philosopher)

The idea

Recording your ideas and insights into a database is a vital step in innovation. Not only will this clarify your ideas, it will allow you to go back and search, cluster, and harvest them too. It can also be extremely useful to revisit your ideas/insights and find that because the environment has changed, they may be workable today.

The ideas bank is different from the ideas wall concept outlined in the previous chapter. While the ideas wall is targeted at capturing your current ideas, the ideas bank comprises all the ideas you have ever had. It is a complete record of your ideas and thoughts.

The ideas bank doesn't have to be complicated and can be as simple as a card index or an Excel spreadsheet. Record each idea along with the date, the need or problem the idea addresses, who will use it (who is the customer) and any factors that need to be in place for the idea to succeed. This last element is probably the most important, so the more specific you can be the better. In the future, a constraint or barrier may be removed and suddenly one of your ideas can be implemented.

Idea	Date	Need	Customer	What needs to be in place 1?	What needs to be in place 2?

Figure 17: Ideas Bank Structure

If you use an Excel spreadsheet, you can organise your ideas using different criteria and then revisit them at least once a month. Many large organisations I have worked for are proficient at generating ideas, but they are not good at storing and reusing them. I have seen so many great ideas being dismissed because their time wasn't right or some market or environmental conditions were not in place.

By setting up the ideas bank, you are preparing the ground for the future – remember the famous saying by ancient Roman philosopher Lucius Annaeus Seneca: luck is "when preparedness meets opportunity." Capturing and recording your ideas is part of being prepared so that when the opportunity arises you are ready to go.

In practice

- Create an Excel spreadsheet to capture your ideas and visit it regularly.

- Print it out and keep it handy.

- Monitor the limiting factors in the environment to see if anything has changed – is the time now right for the idea to be implemented?

PART 4
PROCESS

The process of innovation involves structured action that can be remarkably easy to implement; it typically begins with a problem, or a need, and ends with added value. It is remarkable that so few businesses have actually implemented any innovation process.

60 STAND IN OTHER PEOPLE'S SHOES

"We begin to learn wisely when we're willing to see the world from other people's perspective."

Toba Beta

Figure 18: Other People's Shoes Framework

The idea

We tend to think that everyone thinks like us – we assume the world is as we see it, that everyone has had our experiences.

But the reality is that what you see, hear and feel, may be quite different from what I do. The experiences we have, our family life, our education, all make us who we are. No two individuals have had the same life journey and we all bring our own unique perspective to a problem or idea.

This different perspective is in many cases what makes innovation a reality. The fact that you see things differently may be what allows you to innovate!

Although this divergent viewpoint is useful when you are identifying the opportunity, it can be a negative when you consider the solution. So when you have defined your solution or idea, it is important that you take in others' viewpoint, to make sure what you see is what everyone else sees too.

Take a view from four different perspectives – your customers, stakeholders, employees and competitors. If it is a domestic idea, you can include your children, your partner, your parents, siblings, and an outsider. By forcing yourself to take these other viewpoints, you challenge your preconceptions.

Check your idea out with people you can trust; do they see the value in your idea or solution or do they see barriers?

In practice

- Use the two-by-two framework to check out your idea/solution. Write the idea at the top of a piece of paper and then identify four groups of people who will benefit from it. Think about how they will be affected; how would they view it?

- Write down four people who will be impacted by your idea or solution. Make them real by giving them names and personalities. Think about how they will be affected by your proposal. Look at it from as many angles as you can.

- Envisage a day in the life of one of your four characters. How would your idea affect them? What would be different in their lives because of it?

UNDERSTAND WHAT YOU MEAN BY INNOVATION

"The more you explain it, the more I don't understand it."

Mark Twain

The idea

There are literally thousands of definitions of innovation, so before you start any activity you need to decide what your definition will be. This is important particularly if you are innovating with a large company, as your definition of innovation will be what your activity is measured against.

Types of Innovation

	Insistent	Incremental	Step Change	Changing step	Radical	Disruptive
	doing 'things' for the sake of doing things	doing 'things' differently	doing 'things' very differently	doing different 'things'	changing the way 'things' work	changing what 'things' are
Business Model	Royal Mail	7	Walmart Supply chain optimisation	Apple	iTunes	Wii
Product/ Service	Sony Playstation	FMCG	Smart Car	Apple	Dyson	Amazon Kindle / Nintendo / amazon.com
Process	Royal Mail	HISCOX Insurance	P&G Open Source R&D	iTunes		
Culture	Royal Mail	TOYOTA Kaizen	Virgin			Google

Figure 19: Six Degrees of Innovation

To try and clarify things for a client, I put together the model above which defines six types of innovation – from insistent innovation, where companies just do innovation for the sake of it with no real idea about what they are trying to get out of it, to disruptive innovation, where companies are changing our perceptions and behaviours.

A few examples of these different types of innovation are given in the table below:

Type of innovation	Example company	Rationale for inclusion in this segment
Disruptive innovation	Nintendo	The Nintendo DS and Wii completely turned the video gaming market on its head – different customers, different approach, increased profitability and new markets.
Radical	Dyson Vacuums	Changed the way a vacuum works by removing the need for a dirt bag; traditionally an area where manufacturers had made significant profits.
Changing Step	Apple	Apple moved out of hardware and software and is now making a large proportion of their profits from apps and music through their iTunes service.
Step Change	Virgin	When they entered the airline market, they focused on providing excellent customer service – something that the other airlines failed to do.
Incremental	Microsoft	The Windows product is highly evolutionary with small incremental changes, some of which can be seen as innovative.
Insistent	Most companies	Most companies seem to want to do innovation for innovation's sake with no clear idea of what they are trying to achieve.

Figure 20: Innovation Spectrum Examples

Each of these approaches requires a different strategy, different resources and more importantly, a particular set of criteria to measure success. It is vital that you are honest when you decide which one of these segments your initiative fits in. Too many projects have failed because they were considered radical when really they were incremental!

In practice

- From the thousands of definitions that are out there decide what YOU mean by innovation. If you are working in a company or team, make sure you get a shared understanding. If you don't then you are setting yourself up for failure. If you ask ten people to give you a definition you will get at least eight variations. By getting a shared understanding you will all be working in the same direction.

- Check out the Internet for a variety of definitions from a very diverse collection of people. Choose the one that matches your goals, publish it and try to stick to it.

- Plot your initiative and any other projects you have been involved in on the model. Are all the initiatives in one area? (There is an argument that companies, particularly large ones, should have a portfolio approach to innovation and have something in every box; however, that can lead to dilution of resources if they are in short supply).

- Identify areas where you currently aren't active, and think of what you can do in these areas.

THINK THE UNTHINKABLE

"Discoveries are often made by not following instructions, by going off the main road, by trying the untried."

Frank Tyger

The idea

Many of us have become lazy in the way we think, taking the easy route rather than risking thinking outside the box.

Although this is a low risk approach it can lead to incrementalism, which is not a bad approach though it will not produce the radical innovation ideas which will transform our lives and make breakthroughs in the way we do business.

There are many approaches which you could take to overcome any potential limiting factors in your thinking. They include:

- Challenge – A simple approach is to challenge yourself at each stage of your thinking. Take your idea or solution and look at who the customer will be, how it will be delivered, where the value is, who will benefit, etc. In each of these areas, challenge yourself to come up with at least five different approaches. Once you have these different approaches, think about any new insights you have had and rebuild you idea/solution using some of the new approaches you have defined.

- Deconstruct – When we think about a problem or an idea it is worth deconstructing it as issues that seem insurmountable can become manageable when broken down into component parts. By breaking down your problem or idea, you start to see where you can be different, where you can deliver new value and where you can be truly innovative.

Although these two methods will start you thinking about challenging your preconceptions, it is only a beginning and like many things in life, the more you do it the better you will get at it and the easier it will become.

In practice

- Write down your solution or idea on a sheet of paper and break it down into as many component parts as you can. These should be both tangible and intangible, assets, actions, things that you can control and those you can't control.

- Once you have your breakdown, look for ways that you can do things differently to increase value.

USE RANDOM OBJECTS

"The best way to have a good idea is to have a lot of ideas."

Dr. Linus Pauling

The idea

Take a random object, look at it and use it to see if it sparks any new ideas and associations. This technique has been used successfully for many years to make you think in new ways and create different thoughts. It is an effective way to stimulate insights and help you break out of 'stuck' thinking.

It doesn't really matter what the object is, the more obscure and diverse the better. Look at the shape, the colour, the texture, the proportions and any other factor which you could use to shape your thinking. For each of the elements, think about how it could be linked to your idea.

I find it easier to write down words I associate with the object and then look for possible linkages.

The secret is to think 'openly'. It doesn't matter if the associations are vague and tenuous; sometimes the most obscure association can create the most value.

Once you have your list of associations, try to link them back to your idea or solution. Try using the words you have written down and apply them to stimulate a new thought, a new approach to your problem or a different perspective on your idea.

I find it useful to repeat this process with a few objects and then aggregate all the material I have produced. Then it is time to stand back and take in the whole, rather than focus on the specific words.

The example on the right uses a lemon as the random object and my dog repellent trousers as the idea I want to work on. I have listed some of the words I associate with a lemon on the right of the table, and on the left hand side I have listed how these words can be linked and how they affect my idea. I hope that from this exercise you can see that any object can be used to stimulate ideas and insights.

Yellow	Brightly coloured material
Grow on trees	Grow on trees
Taste tart	Make them taste nasty to dogs
Good for cleaning	Should be easy to clean
Fresh smell	Smell bad to the dog
Dimpled skin	Textured material to deter dogs
Pointed at both ends	Should be close fitting
Contain pips	Have lots of pockets to hold things
Segmented	Segmented knees for easy movement
Thick to protect skin	Thick material around ankles to protect
Imported from hot climate	Made in China?
Always same shape	Fashionable cut
Bought in supermarkets	Market to sell to other people at risk

Figure 21: Random Object Analysis

In practice

- Seek out six random objects you have around the house or office. It really doesn't matter what they are as long as they have some characteristics that you can use to stimulate your thinking.

- An example could be a box of matches. It is brightly coloured on the outside and has a slide-out drawer where the matches are kept. The matches are all pointing in the same direction and can be struck on the side of the box which means this fire-making device is self contained. The matches are made of wood and are uniform in shape and design; and since they have been this shape since they were invented, they are familiar to all generations. As you can see, a simple box of matches has many characteristics which can be used to stimulate thought.

MAP THE PROCESS

"You can't use an old map to see a new land."

Gary Hammel

The idea

Breaking down a process can help you further understand how things work as well as provide you with an opportunity to think about how it can be improved.

The benefits of undertaking this activity are that it can highlight unnecessary steps which can waste time and money.

Creating a map of a process can be an intricate and time-consuming activity, but it can become a valuable tool when complete. A visual representation can be much easier to comprehend than any written procedure.

Understanding the 'big picture' can help people understand what happens across an organisation. Few employees take the time to understand the whole process they are involved in, being happy to just undertake their small part in the organisation. By mapping the process, people can start to understand how their work influences others and it can encourage questioning and challenge. This latter point can lead to significant improvements.

Although this approach may not seem to be particularly innovative, it can provide insights into where a truly innovative approach can be applied – particularly around problem solving.

This technique can be used in a range of situations to identify problems and possible areas for improvement. A more formal version of this approach is used in the Six Sigma approach, which is offered by many consultancies around the world. For further details on the Six Sigma approach check out www.isixsigma.com which is a website dedicated to information on the technique.

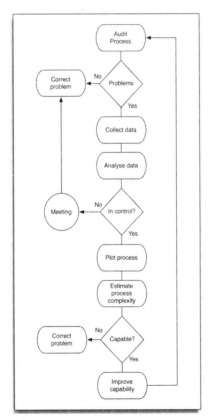

Figure 22: Process Mapping

Note: Be careful not to get too involved in the mapping process as this can divert you from the improvement opportunity.

In practice

- On a large sheet of paper, map out the steps you or your customers, or whoever is going to use or benefit from your idea/solution, can take. Take some time to reflect on your map; talk it through with friends/colleagues. Then do the same thing after your idea/solution has been implemented. Consider if anything has changed because of it; have you simplified things?

- Try using this approach on a wide range of areas. The more you practice the technique, the more ways you will find to use it.

- Create an 'ideal' map of how you would like your life to be. How is this different from what you have today? What would it take to get from one to the other?

65 ALTERNATE BUSINESS MODELS

The idea

Innovation is about looking at things through a different lens, through someone else's eyes or through someone else's business model. To expand your thinking, try thinking about how other companies would run with your idea or how they would implement your solution. By using other business models – EasyJet, Virgin, BA, Apple Nike, etc., you might be able to change your thinking. How would these companies approach your idea or problem?

Look for new insights that will allow you to devise your idea or solution. This exercise will challenge your approach or provide you with a new way of doing things; either way it will increase the chances of your idea or solution being successful. It is not that you are going to adopt these business models, but they may help trigger new thoughts for you.

- An example could be EasyJet. Given their minimal approach to business, they might launch your idea as a 'low-cost' product with the masses as a target market. To allow them to take this approach they would need to strip all the costs out of the equation and brand it quite strongly with the 'Easy' orange logo. They have tried this approach with buses, car rental and hotels. All very basic. Low cost but adequate.

- At the other end of the spectrum is Harrods – how would they approach your idea/solution? Clearly, they address a very different market and style of display, etc. Much of their image is around exclusivity and quality so they would look to position your idea or solution in this style. In this model, costs are not so much an issue; brand image, marketing and celebrity endorsement count for much more. Which celebrity would you use?

- Somewhere in the middle would be a company such as Apple who are known for great design and a model that gives the customer a product or service that is well packaged. This aspirational brand exudes 'cool.' If you look at their business model, they tend not to be leaders but 'fast followers' – bringing their own unique approach to design and customer interface, etc. If Apple were to pick up your idea or solution, how would they approach it?

You can see from the three examples above how you could use this technique to stretch your thinking, maybe redefining your thoughts about which market you want to address, how you could structure your marketing and communication, etc.

In practice

Take four iconic companies and on large sheets of paper write down their mission/vision statements. Under this write down who you think their target market is and what their market entry and growth strategies are. At this stage it doesn't matter if you are wrong; these are your views and they are as valuable as anybody else's.

Once you have your four companies, think about what makes them different – is it a unique approach, leadership, a niche market. Once you have identified their unique points try applying them to your idea/solution.

- How have they done things differently?

- What has made them successful?

- How have they maintained and grown their business?

Lastly, create four new approaches to your idea/solution based on the insights you have gained. Has this changed your thinking?

ABC LEADERSHIP

"Innovation distinguishes between a leader and a follower."

Steve Jobs

The idea

One of the key factors in innovation is the leadership style you have developed over your career.

Maybe your leadership style might not be the best one to get you great results. It may be what is holding you and your idea back. It might be time to try a new approach, to become a new you.

How would you characterise your leadership style? How would others characterise it? Is it autocratic, democratic, strong, leading from the front, from behind...?

To help explore this idea further, you will need to first find other styles. A great way of doing this is to write down a list of leaders of companies or perhaps even countries. I tend to use the alphabet as a guide but you could find others. Try to think laterally, don't just choose leaders who are like you! I have included a table of possible leaders as a guide but you could choose anyone you think is most appropriate. At the side of each leader, write down how you would characterise their leadership style.

Once you have your list of alternate leaders and their styles, pick two or three at random and think about how they would approach your idea. What would they do differently, how would they achieve success? What characteristics have they got that you might want to adopt?

In practice

○ List the alphabet and then think of leaders of countries/ companies who have initials starting with the letters of the alphabet. Pick a few of these at random and then look at how their leadership styles might change things.

- How would they approach your idea/solution?

- How would they measure success?

- How would they extract maximum value from the idea?

- What would they do differently?

○ Map out the particular leader's style in more detail. Identify some of their character traits and then move on to look at their particular leadership style. Once this has been done, it is time to look at how this particular style would change or influence your approach to your idea/solution. This could have a positive or negative effect and it is worth writing this down, as it may be useful later when you come to review your style and how you might adopt/adapt the insights you have gained.

67 EXPLORE THE 'GIVENS'

"In tackling a problem, people commonly assume a set of boundaries to limit the solution. The boundaries of the problem are defined by assumption and then, within those boundaries, conventional thinking is used to find a solution. Very often, however, these boundaries are imaginary, and the solution may lie outside them."

Michael Michalko

The idea

In any situation or when you have any new idea, there will be things that we can change, things that we have some control over and the 'givens' that we have no hope of changing.

Often it is these 'givens', the things we think we cannot change, that can prevent us from moving forward and realising our vision. For instance, let's assume your idea is a new clothes freshness product that means that we don't need to wash our clothes often. Not only will this save water it will also save time. Our clothes will last longer too, which will have a secondary positive impact on the environment as less cotton will be required.

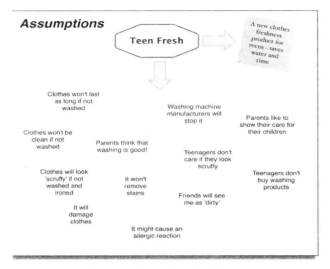

Figure 23: Assumption Analysis

On the right is a map of a few of the assumptions you could make if you were looking at this idea. Although some of these are things that we cannot change, many of the assumptions are not real, they are only perceptions. In reality, these perceptions can be tested with focus groups, and some may turn out to be real blockers for the idea, but the chances are that they will prove to be false.

Figure 24: Assumption Analysis II

The act of writing your assumptions down provides you with many opportunities for innovation. One technique I like is to take each assumption and write at least five ways of overcoming it. On the left, I have taken one of the assumptions 'that teenagers don't wash clothes', and suggested six ways of getting round it.

This technique can be applied to most complex situations where you face obstacles in your path; often the insurmountable barriers that you face can be overcome if only you think laterally.

In practice

Make a list of all the things you think you cannot change – what assumptions are set in concrete?

- For each of these assumptions write down three to five ways you could get around the constraint.

- For those assumptions and constraints that you don't think you can get around, write down who controls it and what you would have to do to change things.

- Now that you have your list of possible alternatives, go over it carefully. Has it changed your thoughts or your approach?

68 MAKE IT REAL – CREATE A MODEL OF YOUR IDEA

"Innovation is the process of turning ideas into manufacturable and marketable form."

Watts Humprey

The idea

One of the biggest challenges in innovation is explaining your vision, your idea or your solution to other people. Because we all see the world differently, we all think differently and take on board ideas and concepts in different ways, the chances of the people you talk to having the same image or understanding of your idea is highly unlikely.

When we explain things to people, we tend to use language and imagery that would work for us. Unfortunately, this may not work for everyone. Our way of understanding is unique to us and this can be a problem when we are trying to describe something new and radical to others.

Many years ago, I was facilitating a group from a major global kitchen appliance manufacturer who wanted to come up with ideas about the future of cooking. The idea of a cooker that was also a fridge was bandied around for a couple of days and although some people kept coming back to the idea, it didn't really progress. I realised that what was being discussed wasn't being envisaged the same way by all the participants. It was clear that there was a distinct lack of understanding; the marketers thought one way, the engineers another and I am sure the CEO had a completely different approach.

It appeared that some people were thinking about a large white box that looked like a fridge and could also cook food, while others visualised a cooker with a chiller unit. We were all using our past experience and knowledge to interpret what was being discussed.

As the idea kept recurring, I decided to try to get everybody to 'see' the same thing so I distributed some cardboard boxes and asked the participants to build a model of what was being talked about.

This led to a frenzy of cutting and sticking card together, and much disagreement about the shape and design of the object. After a couple of hours, a model emerged that everyone was happy with. An hour later, a picture of the model was sent across to the R&D facility in the US and production of a prototype was commissioned.

What I realised from this exercise was that the act of creating a model had aligned everyone's ideas and suddenly there was consensus. The model had become a catalyst and focused people's thoughts; we were now seeing and thinking about the same thing. We were focusing less on what it should be but more about how it could function and how people would use it. The model we built wasn't particularly elegant but it was functional, and was a manifestation of everyone's ideas.

I have used this approach many times on a wide range of topics and ideas, from getting groups to act out a process through website design, to new ideas for products and even marketing campaigns. Making it real and tangible has the effect of aligning the thinking of a group of people, making the task of explaining ideas, concepts and solutions so much easier.

In practice

Take an idea, it doesn't have to be your main idea, just a novel concept or solution, and explain it to a family member or a friend. Do they fully understand the concept? Could they explain it to someone else?

- Next, make it real; build a model from things you have around your home or office. Don't spend too much time or try to make it too sophisticated. Try to explain your idea again using your model. Consider, has this made things easier? Has it changed the conversation? Are people talking about different things?

If your idea is a solution to a problem, try the same technique by getting people to act out the current situation and then your solution. Has this brought new insights to the situation? Has it changed your thoughts about the impact your idea could have?

Try using Lego or Connex to build the model. Maybe get several people to build their idea and then bring them all together into a new form.

69 EXPECT THE UNEXPECTED

The idea

Very often it is the unexpected that derails an idea or solution. Although we can plan for many eventualities, there is always something that cannot be foreseen, or something that we choose to ignore. In his book, *The Black Swan*, Nassim Nicholas Taleb characterises the idea of a Black Swan as: "An event is a surprise (to the observer) and has a major impact. After the fact, the event is rationalised by hindsight."

Most people expect all swans to be white, that is what they have learnt and observed, what their experience tells them. The idea of a black swan is unthinkable, until they see one. A Black Swan event is similar – something that is totally outside the experience of those observing it. Often these events, once they have occurred, are obvious and people create complex explanations for how they occurred and therefore how they could have been predicted. In reality, because similar events had not happened before, the ability to predict them is almost impossible, based on the human mind's inability to conceive the impossible.

In recent months, we have seen a Black Swan event in Japan with the 2011 tsunami which destroyed the Fukushima Nuclear Facility. When the plant was built in the 1950s, detailed planning had gone into its construction and the probability of an earthquake of up to a magnitude of 4 or 5 on the Richter Scale had been taken into account, but no one could predict an offshore quake and the consequential tsunami.

Another significant example is the Arab uprising in 2010/2011, that began when a street vendor in Tunisia set himself alight in December 10, 2010 because he was not allowed to sell his wares. His self-immolation sparked a revolution in Tunisia, which rapidly swept across North Africa and the Middle East, transformed the politics of the region and had repercussions around the world. It was one small act that potentially changed the world.

What can we do to plan for such events?

- The first thing is to not take our current planning too seriously. There has been so much focus on evidential forecasting in the past – we love to create complex predictive spreadsheet models which provide a level of certainty and comfort about our future. Although these are essential for day-to-day planning, they become useless should a Black Swan event hit. I am sure that there were many such systems and forecasts in place at the Fukushima Nuclear Facility and at the World Trade Centre before the attacks on September 11, 2001, 9/11, that proved useless when things went wrong.

- The second thing is to think the unthinkable – what is the worst thing that could happen – what's the next worst thing. I would guess that most people could come up with a list of at least ten things that although improbable, would affect their business should they happen. Lessons from companies such as Shell have shown that having a view about the future and the possible problems it could bring has significant benefit in a turbulent world.

- The third thing is to have a diversity of perspectives when thinking about the future. It is too easy to rely on the same people coming up with the same plan – the Einstein quote about insanity comes to mind – "doing the same thing and expecting different results." Bringing in people with different viewpoints, different experiences and different perspectives can ensure that the unthinkable is thought.

- Lastly, we need to suspend disbelief to experience an alternate reality, a reality where the impossible becomes the possible. Only then can we be ready to face the future head on, without it being a surprise.

In practice

Take time to brainstorm about the things that could throw you off track. Write them down, prioritise them based on impact and scale, and build a workaround for each of the high impact areas.

For each of the ideas, write down their probability (low, medium, high) and their potential impact on your situation (low, medium, high). Focus on the highs and look at how you could mitigate these. What would your strategy be?

LEARN FROM EVERY STEP

"Follow effective action with quiet reflection. From the quiet reflection will come even more effective action."

Peter Drucker

The idea

It is easy to get too embroiled in the day-to-day activities around bringing your idea or solution to reality that we may forget to stand back and just appreciate what has been achieved.

It is useful to reflect on your activities, your achievements and your disappointments because it is only by reflecting in this way that you learn and grow as an individual.

At Toyota, reflection is part of everyday life and Japanese children are taught early on, how to 'perform' reflection, known as the art of Hansei (pronounced *hahn-say*). The true meaning of the word is closer to introspection and Hansei finds its roots in Eastern philosophy and religion.

The key insight is this: "Hansei is performed regularly as a discipline, irrespective of performance! In other words, whether you had a success or failure in your day, you conduct Hansei to better understand the process that led to the specific result."

Often the only time we reflect on a project or initiative is when it fails and we do a post-mortem to find out whom to blame.

The late Peter Drucker was a great advocate of practical reflection. He was fastidious in recording daily in his personal journal, his key decisions and actions, along with an idea of what he thought the outcomes might be. He then reviewed his performance, looking at outcomes and expectations.

Over time, trends show up, revealing strengths and weaknesses. Drucker wrote, "I have been doing this for some 15 to 20 years now. Every time I do it, I am surprised and so is everyone who has ever done this."

This technique is meant to help you improve your performance and creativity by getting your thoughts and actions better aligned, and more importantly making your actions and results more visible to yourself. The hardest part, of course, is the first step which is making time to reflect on the day. Try not to view it as a chore but something to look forward to.

If you use an iPhone, iPad or Android device, there are many cheap programmes that will provide you with a convenient way to record your thoughts. Check out journaling programmes and see which works best for you.

In practice

- Make time in your busy schedule for reflection. I used to travel 30 minutes every day to the office and I would use the journey home to reflect on the day, recording my thoughts on a small voice recorder.

- Keep a daily journal of what you have achieved, what you have learnt that day, and what has surprised you. As you look back on your experience, it is easy to forget how far you have come and how much you have learnt and discovered about yourself.

- Build on your achievements and learn from any disappointments.

- Spot trends. As time progresses (and after you've done this for a while), note any recurring themes and write down any potential connections among seemingly unconnected things.

71 ANTICIPATE PROBLEMS, OBSTACLES, ENEMIES AND PROCESSES

"Once we rid ourselves of traditional thinking we can get on with creating the future."

James Bertrand

The idea

One of the secrets of successful innovation is to understand in detail the environment you are trying to operate in. There are many things that can halt a great idea or solution, and although it is impossible to identify all the possible pitfalls, it is worth trying to identify as many as you can, as early as you can, so you can put strategies in place to overcome them.

Overcoming Obstacles

Many people see obstacles as a setback, an attack on their idea or in some cases themselves. In reality, obstacles are just a way of getting feedback from reality, a way of showing you that you need to adjust your strategy and refine the way you are executing it. Interestingly, obstacles can be one of your best friends as they encourage you to innovate in new ways to overcome them. Every obstacle is an opportunity to find a new way, to innovate!

Our minds often do not distinguish between a real and imagined thought, and one great way to overcome obstacles is to imagine a situation where you have successfully overcome the obstacle.

Assume that you had no constraints, no barriers, everyone was out to help you and you couldn't fail. Once you have created this vision, ask yourself how you got there, who helped you and how you overcame the barriers. Don't rush at this task, give yourself time to think, to ponder. You will be amazed at some of the ideas you come up with.

It is worth trying to involve as many people as you can in this activity, as they will all bring different perspectives on the situation. If you try it alone, you will only have your ideas, your personal experience to draw on. Involving others brings their knowledge and experiences to the table, which can spark new ideas and insights.

Dealing with enemies

When I talk about enemies, I mean people who will try to stop you achieving your goals, those who try to knock your self-confidence and are generally unhelpful. Dealing with these people can be a chore. One of the challenges is that this negativity can be contagious, and you may find that it quickly spreads from one person to a whole group.

One approach is to find people who are positive and supportive, and surround yourself with them rather than the naysayers. Although this is an effective way to go, it can get a bit sycophantic and 'stale.' As one of the keys to successful innovation is access to a diverse range of opinions and insights, this approach can be restrictive.

My own approach is to have a clear vision of what you are trying to achieve. If you have this vision and the passion to succeed, then you can conquer any amount of negativity.

One thing I have found that works well is to give the doubters a task or a challenge. Turn their negative comments into questions that force them to think about your idea or solution in new ways. If they claim that customers won't buy the product, ask them, 'What would

I have to do to make the proposition attractive to the customer?' or 'Who do you think the customer would be?' By getting them involved in your initiative, you can turn them into your supporters rather than your enemies.

Note: Often the biggest barrier to success is you! We can be our own worst enemies, and we impose limitations and boundaries on ourselves with our negative self talk. Whenever you come across a problem or a potential barrier, instead of thinking about the impact it will have, think about five ways of getting around it – turn the negative into a positive.

In practice

Identify as many things as you can that will potentially stop or delay your idea/solution. Once you have your list, categorise it and think about ways of addressing each issue.

- Mind-mapping can be an effective way of visually capturing this list. You can do this physically using post-it notes or on one of the many computer applications available.

It is useful to involve as many people as you can in this exercise as their perspective may be different from yours, and therefore they will have different ideas.

Make sure you have a clear vision about what you are trying to achieve, and what 'great' would look like. This will keep you focused.

Prepare a few questions you can fire back at the naysayers to get them involved.

FEED ON FAILURE

The idea

Take a look at your problem or opportunity; what hasn't worked and try to turn the negative into positive.

Failure seems to be in vogue at the moment, with 'fail fast' being the watchword in many innovation activities. This focus on failure can be a real barrier though, when dealing with innovation. We should instead talk about learning or discovery. Failure is simply one element in creating new knowledge and learning.

The Thomas Edison quote at the top of the page sums it up for me in that he didn't fail, he just learnt what wouldn't work. If he had given up at the first hurdle, he would never have invented the light bulb and our world would probably be very different today, certainly darker!

When talking to someone about a new idea or solution they have, I like to use the phrase "If you absolutely couldn't fail what would you do?" When you do this with a group it is surprising that often people respond very quickly with enthusiasm and passion for whatever it is that they want to do.

The reality is that the fear of failure is often the only thing holding people back – a self-limiting belief system that we have developed and built up in our lives.

If you take the time to look back at your early life, you will find that it is filled with failure, beginning with the time you fell over as a toddler learning to walk. But this isn't really failure, it is learning. The question really is: At what point or age does learning become failure?

In our childhood, we have an innate curiosity for all things and we unconsciously employ a problem solving strategy which we refine and use throughout our lives, although as we get older the emphasis changes. We start by Questioning, we then Hypothesise the options, we Experiment and lastly we Reflect.

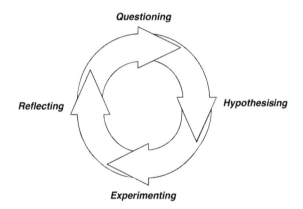

Figure 25: Problem Solving Cycle

As a child we focus on the questioning and experimentation phases and in later life this focus changes to the hypothesise and reflection stages. This change in emphasis leads to inaction. A child, on the other hand, hasn't had the experiences which allow for much hypothesising or reflection, they just question and try out new things.

The secret to dealing with the perception of failure is to become more childlike in our approach; bring balance back to the four phases and see each outcome as a learning that we can build upon.

"Virtually nothing comes out right the first time. Failures, repeated failures, are signposts on the road to achievement. The only time you don't want to fail is the last time you try something. One fails toward success."

Charles Kettering

In practice

* When you are faced with failure ask "What worked, what didn't, and why?". It is just as important to understand what doesn't work as what does. Once you have identified what didn't work, write down three or five things that you could have done differently to change the outcome.

PART 5
RESEARCH

Research is an important factor when considering innovation. The more information and stimulation you have, the more opportunities there will be for building linkages between ideas and thoughts.

73 SET UP A BLOG

"A blog is merely a tool that lets you do anything from changing the world to sharing your shopping list."

Anonymous

The idea

Over the last few years, we have seen the impact of social networking change the way we think, behave and live our lives. At the end of 2010, there were over 150 million blogs on the Internet, 175 million people on Twitter and over 600 million people on Facebook (Source: www.royal.pingdom.com). This massive growth in online social activity has led to changes in the way companies approach innovation, with Open Innovation and Crowdsourcing now on the agenda of many of the large organisations around the world.

So how can you effectively participate in this new wave of activity? Setting up a blog can be a great way of getting new ideas and finding new contacts.

There are a number of approaches you could take when considering an Innovation Blog:

- Reputation/Relationship building – position yourself as an 'expert' in the field and promote new ideas and concepts, as well as your skills and capabilities. In this model, you will gather a following for your blog, and your followers will keep track of your ideas and any new developments. One of the disadvantages is that this can be an onerous approach, as you have to keep your blog fresh and generate new material to satisfy your readers, or they will disappear and find new sites to follow. On the positive side, this can be an opportunity to generate new income streams from advertisers.

- Research and idea gathering – using a blog as a way of generating and researching new ideas can be an effective way of gaining insights. This approach relies on you creating content that people will want to discuss, not always an easy thing to do, although get it right and it can generate some interesting insights. The possible downside to this approach is the question of intellectual property. If you use an idea from a blog that someone else has generated, then there is a question about who owned the idea, and if there is any financial benefit to be gained from the idea, how will it be handled.

- Community building – this is probably the most productive approach although initially it can be difficult to get started. The concept here is to find a group of people who are interested in a particular approach or idea. Although similar to the previous approach, this concept relies on the 'open' way to idea generation, similar to Linux, where intellectual property is generated for the common good. The secret here is to get other people to start blogging as well as yourself. This generates more interest in your blog and takes the pressure off you to generate material every day. An example here is www. openinnovators.net, which is a community of people who are interested in the topic of open innovation.

- Journaling activity – this is the approach that many blogs take. It is a simple journal of activities and insights that spring up from everyday activity.

- News and information – providing people with information about what is happening in the field of innovation is another approach which you could take. This relies on you having a finger on the pulse of the industry, or access to material that others don't have. A good example is http://creativityandinnovation.blogspot.com/ a site which provides examples of good innovation on the Internet.

- Opinion/comment/controversy – there are many examples of this type of site though they don't have a regular following. The benefit is that they can gain high profile, sometimes for the wrong reasons, but do provide an opportunity to generate income from advertising, etc.

All the above approaches are valid and it may be that you have to try more than one before you settle on the right one for you. The most important thing is to get started. I suggest that you start with a journal site to get into the habit of writing on a daily/weekly basis, and build from there. It is good if you can get comments and conversations started on the site, as this will attract more people, so pose a question at the end of a blog post, or ask for comments.

Once you have established your blog, you can think about your strategy. Think about what you want to get out of the blog and what success would look like. This will help you decide which approach to take. The next area to consider is marketing your blog. How are you going to let people know about it and how are you going to attract people? It may be that you choose to simply email all your contacts, or maybe take a more aggressive approach and pay for marketing. Whichever route you take, as with any marketing, it is important to measure your success: What are you putting in, in terms of cost, time, effort, and what are you getting out in terms of visits, revenue, etc.

The key to a popular blog is to think about your readers when posting entries. Who are you targeting, and what does your potential audience expect from you?

Don't forget that getting visitors to your site is not only good for you, it can also be monetised through entities like Amazon Associates where you can recommend books and get a percentage of the price of any books bought, through to programmes such as BlogAds which allows you to choose the advertising you have on your site as well as collect payments, etc.

In practice

- There are a number of websites which offer blogs at no cost if you are prepared to put up with some advertising. Try these first and if you like blogging then move onto a paid service. Check out www.blogger.com, www.typepad.com to start with.

  - Start by documenting your day or week, pulling out any innovation insights you may have had or lessons that you have learnt. This will get you into the habit of blogging and test if people are interested in what you are writing about.

  - Once you have established your blog, a good way to find your direction is to conduct a survey using a website such as www.surveymonkey which allows you to undertake a study of up to 100 people which should be enough to start with.

- Keep your blog up to date – post at least once a week or people will start to move away from it. It may be that you only write a couple of lines but it will keep it fresh in the 'bloggershere.'

- Link your blog to your Facebook page and your LinkedIn page to get more visitors

If you go to a conference, it is worth blogging whilst you are there, as this can attract large numbers of visitors – at TED a couple of years ago, I blogged from the conference and went from 80 readers a week to over 5,000!

Keep reviewing your blog; check if it is still interesting. Are you getting any comments? What can you do to make it better?

Lastly, don't forget to look at the possibility of monetising the site through advertising or associate programmes.

COMPETITIVE ANALYSIS

"A focus on cost-cutting and efficiency has helped many organisations weather the downturn, but this approach will ultimately render them obsolete. Only the constant pursuit of innovation can ensure long-term success."

Daniel Muzyka

The idea

It is important to understand what your competition is doing. Although you may think you have a unique idea or solution, the reality is that there may be something similar out there already.

This is increasingly important since the Internet has created a global marketplace for products and services; an idea or product can spread around the world in seconds, and be copied with little respect for copyright and patent.

When thinking about your potential or real competition, it is vital to first understand who it is. It used to be relatively simple to find someone offering a similar product or service; all you had to do was to talk to your prospective customers. Although this is still a good approach, you may find that the answer you get isn't what you expected as companies and individuals nowadays often turn to the Internet and sites such as eBay, to source products and services.

The first thing to do is a simple Internet search. This can seem daunting, but it is amazing what you can glean just by trying a few searches in one search engine such as Google. You can also try one of the search engine aggregators such as Dogpile.com, which uses many of the search engines and aggregates the results.

	You	Competitor A	Competitor B
Name			
Key competitor strength			
Market size			
Customer base			
Funding source (From reports and accounts)			
Implied strategy			
Trajectory	↗↓ → ↗ ↘	↗↓ → ↗ ↘	↗↓ → ↗ ↘

Figure 26: Competitor Analysis Framework

Once you have identified your competitive landscape, the next step is to refine your search down to the closest three or four companies. If the companies are publicly listed (Ltd. or LLC) then Reports and Accounts are filed and should be available online. These can be a valuable source of information – particularly about strategy, funding, staffing, etc. Try to complete the framework above for these companies. This should help you focus your thoughts about who your competition is – but, more importantly, what their competitive advantage might be.

This initial competitive analysis is just the beginning and as your ideas grow, and your initiative evolves, you will need to revisit this analysis on a regular basis. Who you think your competitor is today may not be your competitor tomorrow.

One consideration when looking at competition is copyright and patents. The question of how you are going to protect your idea will be fundamental to your success. This is particularly relevant if you are developing a new product or service. My advice is to write down in detail your idea or solution and lodge it with a solicitor. This way you can prove the provenance of the idea as well as the date and time.

The second consideration is the protection of your idea/solution when pitching it to a company – whether they are a prospective customer or partner. Before you go ahead with this, it is worth getting them to sign a non-disclosure document drawn up by someone who understands the law in the country you will be pitching in. This differs from country to country. A Google search will reveal sample non-disclosure agreements as well as resources and companies that can help you protect your idea.

In the end, the best way to protect yourself is by being extra cautious about who you share your idea with. It's worth talking extensively with others in your industry, and getting referrals before disclosing your concept to anyone.

In practice

- Try searching the Internet using a website such as dogpile.com which aggregates a wide range of search engines and consolidates the results.

  - Try to think laterally when compiling your search terms; don't just type in the first thing that comes to you or you may miss something.

  - Ask others to help you in your search; they may use different search strategies and elicit new information.

- Revise your list of competitors to identify your top three. For each of these companies try to complete the framework in this chapter.

- Once you have your list of competitors, think about their key competitive strengths; how does your idea/solution measure up to them? Is it different enough?

75 APPLY CONSTRAINTS

"Wealth flows directly from innovation... not optimisation... wealth is not gained by perfecting the known."

Kevin Kelly

The idea

This is a technique where you impose false constraints to get the innovation 'juices' flowing. We get lazy in our thinking sometimes, and when we try to think up new things, we tend to start from where we are today. Although this is a valid approach, it often leads to incremental change and not transformational change.

At the opposite end of the spectrum is the blank canvas, which while providing limitless possibilities for a new product or solution, often proves difficult at the start. If we really need to think creatively, we need to have some boundaries. The idea of limitless opportunities (or a blank canvas) causes our brains to go into overload. In reality, we are not really creators but adapters, we enjoy figuring out how to fix things, not necessarily creating something new.

If we take the approach that innovation isn't really about creation, but rather about finding solutions to existing problems, then we have already introduced constraints into our thinking. Clearly defining the customer, the need or the problem starts to build constraints into our thinking. The trick is to introduce too many constraints as this really can stifle innovation and creativity.

When thinking about constraints, try not to be limited to the obvious. Start with a need, a market, a customer, a problem. Once you have this clearly defined, try applying constraints to the topic:

- How could we do it for half the price
- Make it half the size
- Use different material
- Half the staff
- Twice as quick

The first response to these questions is usually "it can't be done", "it's impossible". However, this approach encourages people to think harder and be more innovative, and usually after a few hours or maybe even days, the solution or idea pops up.

A great example of this approach is the One Laptop Per Child idea that Nicholas Negroponte proposed in 2006. The concept was to build a laptop for $100 that every child in the world could use. Initially the idea was ridiculed and thought to be impossible. With laptops at the time costing over $100, the idea of a $100 laptop seemed ridiculous. The constraint of $100 drove a whole industry to rethink what a laptop was and that people should be able to use it. The result was a laptop that didn't cost $100 but came in at $199.

Although the original dream of providing every child in the world with a laptop has not yet been achieved, the project has fueled research into lowering the cost of laptops and is credited with the birth of the low cost netbook we see today. This radical change to the technology landscape was driven from one major constraint being applied to the field of laptop technology – the $100 constraint.

Constraints alone can stifle and kill innovation and creativity. This can lead to a feeling of pessimism and despair. So, while we need constraints to fuel passion, innovation and insight, we also need optimism to keep us engaged and focused on finding the right idea or solution.

"It is from the interaction between constraint, and the disregard for the impossible that unexpected insights, cleverness, and imagination are borne."

Marissa Ann Mayer, Google

Innovation is the art of finding the constraint that is going to drive new insights and ideas.

In practice

Once you have your idea or solution, try applying the following constraints:

- How could we do this for half the cost?
- How could we double the benefit without incurring additional cost?
- How could we deliver it with half the resources?
- How could we make it half the size without affecting capability?

One area where you can try this concept out is photography. Try taking your camera out one day with the objective of taking an outstanding photograph and see what you get. The next time you go out, apply a constraint to your photography, for instance a specific building or subject, such as a window or an animal. You will probably find the second exercise more rewarding and it will make you think about what you are photographing.

NO CONSTRAINTS

"Creativity requires the courage to let go of certainties."

Erich Fromm

The idea

Taking away all the constraints that could stop you is a great way of realising what you could achieve. We naturally apply constraints, developed over time through learning and experience, to our thinking. These may be real or assumed and typically, these are the basis of the way we operate on a day-to-day basis. These constraints could be personal, such as what you think you are capable of, or business oriented such as what you think will work and what won't. Even the word innovation can be a constraint as it provides a 'box' to put our idea or solution into.

It is interesting that it is these notional constraints that often prevent us from enjoying new experiences in our lives. The difference in the most successful business leaders is that at some point in their lives, they redefined or realigned their perception of their constraints.

So, what if you had no constraints, if nothing was holding you back, you absolutely could not fail, what would you do, how would you do it and most importantly what would the result be? This can be a hard path to follow as we have been building our constraints model for a long time and it is embedded in our psyche at some deep level.

It can, however, be a very liberating exercise to try as it can have a fundamental impact, not just on your innovation activities but on the rest of your life as well.

The first step is to create a vision of success for your idea or solution. What would a perfect world look like? This is not easy, as your thinking will be conditioned by what exists today, so it is worth starting with a blank sheet of paper. I have included an example worksheet in the 'In Practice' section below.

As Nike says, *'Just Do It.'*

"... if I could not fail"

What would a typical day be like?	How would I know if I had achieved my dream?

Write a best selling book on travel which would fund my travel and vacations for the rest of my life

Who helped me achieve my dream?	What resources would I need?

What are the three things stopping me from achieving my goal?	What are the three things I need to do to overcome them?
1	1
2	2
3	3

Figure 27: No Constraints Framework

In practice

- Use the framework in Figure 27 and on a sheet of paper write at the top – "... if I could not fail".

- In the middle of the sheet, write your idea, solution or dream.

- Around the outside write down what a typical day would be like for either yourself or someone affected by the idea/solution. Next write down what your success criteria would be – try to make this both tangible (money) and intangible (feelings). Third, write down what resources you would need to achieve your goal, and lastly, assume that the goal has been reached. Write down who helped you achieve it.

- On the example sheet above, I have also included a section to write down your three top constraints and three ways to get around them. This is a useful exercise as it may get you thinking about how significant, or not, they may be.

77 CONSIDER THE BIG PICTURE

"Never before in history has innovation offered promise of so much to so many in so short a time."

Bill Gates

The idea

Our natural reaction when we think of a new idea or solution is to quickly get down to the practicalities of delivering it, marketing it and most of all, making something happen. This activity can become all consuming and we forget sometimes to stand back and consider the bigger picture – the context for our idea or solution.

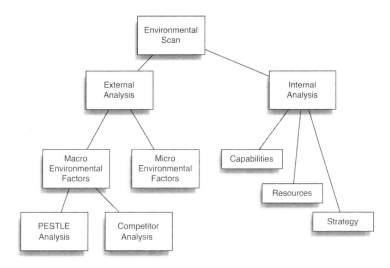

Figure 28: The Big Picture

It is worth taking time to understand the wider context of your idea or problem. Don't be constrained by what you know; use all the tools available to paint a picture of the wider landscape.

A great example of this is Nintendo with their Wii games system. The industry and their major competitors, Sony and Microsoft, were in a battle for higher graphics, games that were more complex, and faster processors, which Nintendo probably couldn't win. The traditional target for these games was a 16 – 23 old male, and the games typically took many weeks to understand and master, also playing them was a solitary affair.

Nintendo, which roughly translated means 'leave luck to heaven', stood back, looked at the context for the game console and identified that the traditional consoles were typically situated in a separate room where people went to play, taking them away from family time. Other people in the house, namely the mother and smaller children, weren't being served by the games industry.

In a radical move, they launched the Nintendo DS aimed at this new market sector of mothers and smaller children. Their premise was that the games had to have a social element where groups of people could interact. The result was very positive for the company; they seemed to have hit a new 'sweet spot' for gaming. On the back of this success, they introduced the Wii console which was clearly aimed at all members of the family and had a very high social context, being adopted by all members of the family as well as institutions such as Weight-watchers.

The strategy brought gaming out of the bedroom and into the lounge, and brought families together. The result was a dramatic increase in sales, doubling the company's market share from less than 30% in 2007, to over 65% in 2010, which left its competitors struggling to keep up. Had Nintendo not taken a wider look at the market, it would have remained on the 'technology escalator,' trying to keep up with the bigger, better funded rivals. Instead, by taking a fresh look at the big picture, it single-handedly managed to reshape the games console market and its fortunes.

Sometimes we need to lift our eyes and see what's around us; when we are too focused on the trees, we forget we are in a forest.

In practice

* There are many tools which can be used to map out the bigger picture, and your resources, budget and the scope of your idea/solution will direct how much effort you put into this. Figure 29 below provides a framework for you to use. On the left are the six categories that are typically used when looking at the bigger picture; once the factors have been identified in these categories, a SWOT analysis can be undertaken to identify which one will have the most impact on you or your company.

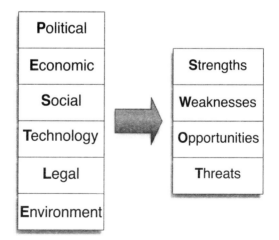

Figure 29: PESTLE and SWOT Frameworks

- Environmental scan. This is typically a broad look at the environment you are looking to operate in, or are involved in. This would then lead to an internal and external look at this environment.

- The most commonly used analysis is the PESTLE framework:

  - Political – includes government regulations, tax, employment law, trade restrictions as well as the political agenda and how this might change.

  - Economic – includes economic forecasts, interest rates, inflation predictions which will all affect the buying power of customers and the cost of capital, etc.

  - Social – includes factors such as population growth, demographics, health and attitudes to work and life.

  - Technology – these factors are becoming increasingly important from both a consumer and business viewpoint. This should include both current and future technologies which may have an impact on your idea or solution.

  - Legislative – What legal and regulatory issues may be relevant to your idea or solution.

  - Environment – This is a recent factor but one which is becoming increasingly important. Issues here include the carbon impact of your idea or solution as well as recycling, etc.

- Once you have undertaken the PESTLE analysis, the next step is to look at the Strengths, Weaknesses, Opportunities and Threats of your idea/solution. Then see how you can build on your Strengths, turn Weaknesses into Strengths and turn Threats into Opportunities.

78 · CREATE A VISION FOR YOUR IDEA

"Once again, this nation has said there are no dreams too large, no innovation unimaginable and no frontiers beyond our reach."

John S. Herrington

The idea

When we have ideas or solutions to problems, we typically base them on our everyday life in the present. The challenge is to understand how the environment for the idea or solution will evolve over time. It is no good solving a problem or need today that will go away in six months time due to some other factor such as government legislation or a new technology or service. Looking into the future is key to successful innovation – understanding how the future landscape will evolve and setting a goal will give you the edge when it comes to developing your idea or solution.

Creating a vision is the first step in the process of business:

1. Vision: what do you want the outcome of your idea or solution to be in five years?

2. Goals: create the framework to achieve your vision.

3. Objectives: create measurable terms such as how you will know when you have achieved your vision.

4. Tasks: how will the objectives be accomplished; who will do what and when?

5. Timelines: when will they be accomplished?

6. Follow-up and review, monitoring goals and objectives.

Note: Items two to four in the list above are what is generally included in a strategy and items five and six are typically considered part of a business plan.

Often vision statements are confused with mission statements. While mission statements guide an organisation in its day-to-day operations, outlining values and ways of working, visions provide a sense of direction and purpose in the long term, the means of moving towards the future.

It must be said though, that creating and articulating the vision is relatively easy, it is the execution that is the hard part. In 1961 when Kennedy articulated the vision of putting a man on the moon by the end of the decade, it was a simple thing to say. The hard part was the actual accomplishment of the vision, and yet setting a clear and simple vision inspired a generation, and as it turned out, the goal was achieved.

The ability to create, articulate and 'live' the vision is what sets leaders apart from managers.

"Managers are people who do things right and leaders are people who do the right thing. The difference may be summarised as activities of vision and judgment – effectiveness verses activities of mastering routine – efficiency."

Warren Bennis and Burt Nanus (2007)

It is important that any vision you create is Believable, Attractive and Realistic for people to buy into it, so that they want to help you achieve it. It should also be set in the future to provide a direction for people to head towards. Going back to the space programme, I like the story of Apollo 13 – they had a clear and believable vision of what they were aiming for, the moon, which allowed them to correct their course. I am not sure if the story is apocryphal, but it is a good metaphor nevertheless, for the need for a vision.

In practice

- Create a vision for your idea or solution, make sure it's at least five years out to paint a picture of what you are trying to achieve or solve, making things better than they are today. Make sure your vision is believable, realistic and attractive so that people will want to buy into it. Check it with family and friends; does it excite them?

Example Vision Statements:

- Avon Cosmetics – "To be the company that best understands and satisfies the product, service and self-fulfillment needs of women globally"

- Caterpillar – To be the global leader in customer service

- The Coca-Cola Company Mission:

  - To refresh the world in mind, body and spirit

  - To inspire moments of optimism through our brands and actions

  - To create value and make a difference everywhere we engage

- Kraft Foods – "Helping People around the World Eat and Live Better."

- RSPCA – "To work for a world in which all humans respect and live in harmony with all other members of the animal kingdom."

- Royal National Institute for the Deaf (RNID) – Our vision is a world where deafness and hearing loss are not barriers to opportunity and fulfillment.

PLAN FOR ACTION

"Failing to plan is planning to fail."

Alan Lakein

The idea

If you want to maximise the creativity of the ideas you generate and ensure the best ones are implemented, you need a plan. It is relatively easy to have the idea in the first place but more than 99% of great ideas fail because there isn't a plan to deliver it. A plan forms part of an overall structured way of thinking about your idea. Many documents and books offer ways of planning, and frameworks.

To help put the plan into context, I have provided a structure I have developed over the years when approaching a new idea or initiative. It is not essential that you have all these elements, but having this structure at least makes you think about them and consider what value they would add to helping you achieve your idea/solution.

The first step of your plan is to state the idea or problem in a sentence – make it clear, concise and understandable. Next, you need to consider how involved you are going to be – are you simply preparing a proposal for management or are you going to manage the complete project yourself?

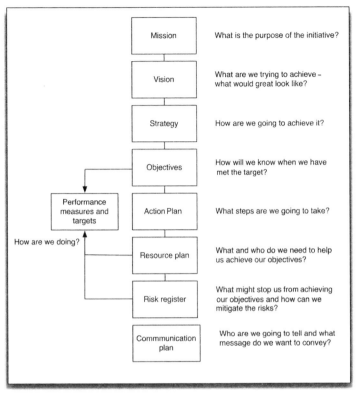

Mission		What is the purpose of the initiative?
Vision		What are we trying to achieve – what would great look like?
Strategy		How are we going to achieve it?
Objectives		How will we know when we have met the target?
Performance measures and targets	Action Plan	What steps are we going to take?
How are we doing?	Resource plan	What and who do we need to help us achieve our objectives?
	Risk register	What might stop us from achieving our objectives and how can we mitigate the risks?
	Commmunication plan	Who are we going to tell and what message do we want to convey?

Figure 30: Action Plan

It is important at this stage to be realistic about your skills, capabilities and time. Although we all think we can do most things, in reality, we are probably good at only some. It may be easier to try to do as much as we can ourselves – and this will also reduce the cost – but in reality it may cost more and have less likelihood of success.

Your plan doesn't have to be complex but it should outline the key activities you think you will need to undertake.

Having a plan also lets you track your idea/solution and monitor your performance, allowing you to focus on the important things rather than getting distracted by non-issues that demand your time and attention. At this stage, it is also worth documenting any risks and dependencies that may have an impact on your plan, and thinking about the people you will need to recruit to help you achieve your goal.

Lastly is the thorny issue of communicating your plan; who do you tell, and how much do you reveal? This will depend on what your idea/solution is and whether you feel confident enough to bring other people onboard.

In practice

- Create an action plan for your idea/solution – make it realistic and keep it up to date. Undertake regular reviews of the plan and seek comments on progress.

  - Document risks, dependencies.

- Create a communication plan for your idea/solution. It doesn't need to be detailed but should include who you will be communicating to and what message you want to get across.

80 AMPLIFICATION THROUGH SIMPLIFICATION

"... it is always the simple that produces the marvelous."

Amelia Barr

The idea

When we get that brilliant idea or solution, the temptation is to build on it, adding new features and frills. The excitement of the insight/idea sparks our creative juices and it can be difficult to stop improving things. The problem with this approach is that we lose focus and get distracted.

Although it is always good to improve on an idea or solution, the activity can prevent us from delivering the original idea. The key to successful innovation, which is not just about having a great idea but delivering it and extracting value from it, is to keep it simple. The more complex you make it the less likely you are to succeed.

For many years I have been an advocate of the work of Scott McCloud. In his book *Understanding Comics* he talks about the technique comic artists use to make the complex understandable. It is through this abstract illustration that McCloud is able to make palatable a topic which otherwise could be heavy and difficult to digest. He calls this 'amplification through simplification'. "When we abstract an image... we are not so much eliminating details as we are focusing on specific details. By stripping down an image to its essential meaning, an artist can amplify that meaning."

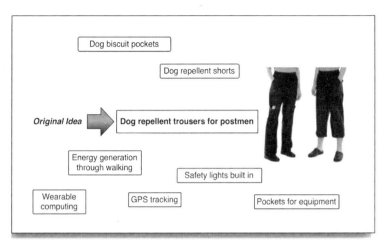

Figure 31: Dog Repellent Trousers Concept

Taking this concept of amplification through simplification and applying it to innovation is a good discipline.

The simpler you can make your idea the easier it is to explain to people, the more likely you are to get the support you need.

In the example on the right for 'Dog Repellent Trousers for post persons,' it would be easy to get distracted by the idea of embedding some sort of technology into the trousers. Researching the technology and looking at the how and what this would be, could easily distract you from just delivering a basic dog repellent garment. Despite the fact that the technology might be more interesting than looking at fabrics and fit, it probably isn't where the most value would be gained. Although some of the other ideas could be good add-ons, later investigating them would probably mean that you never developed the original trouser idea in the first place.

In practice

- Write you main idea down on a sheet of paper and pin it to your desk or somewhere you can see it on a regular basis; keep it simple and understandable. This should keep you focused on what you are trying to achieve.

- On a separate sheet of paper, write your main idea in the centre and all your other ideas that build on it around it. Look to group these ideas and then rank them on value and ease of implementation. Keep revisiting this paper, adding to it, refining it and reviewing it, but don't let it distract you from the main task in hand, which is delivering your main idea!

PART 6
TECHNIQUE

There are many different techniques and tools which can help you in your innovation initiatives. Choose the technique which best suits you and allows you to achieve your goal.

MOST RIDICULOUS IDEAS

"I once knew a chap who had a system of just hanging the baby on the clothes line to dry and he was greatly admired by his fellow citizens for having discovered a wonderful innovation on changing a diaper."

Damon Runyon

The idea

Don't dismiss seemingly stupid ideas, they may seem ridiculous now, but they may be brilliant in a different situation.

There are many examples of remarkable ideas that have made people serious money. For example, the Snuggie, which has made an estimated $200m in profit since its 'inventor,' Scott Boilen, came up with the idea of putting a bathrobe on backwards, a seemingly ridiculous idea which was transformed into a multimillion dollar business venture.

Another of my favourites is the Doggles – goggles for dogs. Dogs don't need goggles and never have but the ridiculous idea caught on in the US and Australia and has made the inventors, Ken and Roni di Lullo, millions of dollars. The product now sells in 16 countries and is being used by the US military in Iraq and Afghanistan. The goggles have been deployed to protect military dogs' eyes from dust and strong sunlight. This seemingly crazy idea has now spawned a whole industry providing accessories for dogs.

Both these ideas started out as 'silly' but they addressed an unmet need which has turned their inventors into multimillionaires. It would have been easy to dismiss these ideas as ridiculous and put them to one side, but by keeping them simple, delivering a product and some clever marketing, they won through.

In Japan in 1997, Kenji Kawakami introduced the term *Chindogu* that translated means unusual. In a regular article in the *Tokyo Journal*, readers were invited to send in ideas that solved problems but in an unusual way. What emerged was a whole host of what on the surface seemed ridiculous ideas, which had an element of reality in them. *Chindogu* ideas had to conform to three basic elements: they had to be able to be made, they had to be in the public domain (not have a patent outstanding), and lastly they had to have some element of reality and not only be made for the purpose of humour. A book *101 Unuseless Japanese Inventions: The Art of Chindogu* published in 1995 has sold over half a million copies worldwide. Search on the Internet for *Chindogu* and see if the images and ideas provide any insight.

This technique can be a great way of getting out of 'stuck thinking', that point in your project or initiative where you meet a roadblock, a seemingly insurmountable problem or barrier to moving forward.

We all have crazy thoughts from time to time, the difference is that we quickly dismiss them instead of thinking them through and doing something about them.

The next time you have a seemingly ridiculous idea write it down, think about it, maybe discuss it with family and friends. After they stop laughing you may discover you have a multimillion dollar business venture!

In practice

* Write down the three craziest ideas you can come up with. One way to start looking for some inspiration is by searching the web for the word *Chindogu*. There are many examples here of seemingly crazy solutions to everyday problems; maybe one of them will stimulate some insight for you.

  • Once you have your list of three crazy ideas, start by thinking about your marketing plan. What would an advertisement look like for your idea? Which celebrity would you get to endorse it?

  • Now that you have your marketing plan, who would the customer be and how would you go about producing the product or service?

  • Lastly, reflect on the idea, is it really crazy or is there a kernel of brilliance in there?

WORK BACKWARDS

"The most effective way to cope with change is to help create it."

I. W. Lynett

The idea

Most of the time when we start thinking about an idea or solution we begin with a current problem or situation and work forward in small steps, taking an incremental approach. Although this approach is valid, it is unlikely to lead to radical innovation or significant disruption of the status quo.

One approach to thinking differently is to start at the end; rather than think forward, think backwards. An oft cited example of this is the story of the 'horse buggy whip' story. As cars replaced horse-drawn carriages, buggy whip manufacturers tried improving quality, reducing costs, and consolidating market share. Of course, it didn't save them. It is no good trying to improve on your idea or solution if your entire niche is obsolete.

It can be seen that the buggy whip manufacturers were taking a typical incremental view; instead of trying to improve their product they could have looked at a world without horses and what they could produce for this new environment.

Even today, the buggy whip story can be played out with computer manufacturers. They spent much of the 1990s tweaking and changing the laptops that we all lugged around – making them faster, with bigger screens and higher resolution graphics. This strategy worked until Nicholas Negroponte came along and proposed the $100 laptop. The traditional manufacturers laughed and said it couldn't be done but within two years the dream of a $100 laptop had been achieved, well almost, and the people who had laughed at the notion suddenly found themselves in a new world, rapidly trying to catch up with the new low-cost netbook market which had been spawned from this one idea.

Rather than work from the current technology platform, the suppliers who were involved in the $100 laptop project had to create new technologies, new operating systems and new storage technologies to meet the demands of the project. By working backwards, a whole new industry was created.

A second example is the Tesla car. The problem with the hybrid drive train has always been the size and weight of the battery.

Tesla's approach was to work backwards from a car that would go from 0 – 60 in less than four seconds and travel for more than 200 miles before it required refueling/recharging. The solution the company came up with was a completely different approach to batteries. Rather than have a single battery pack, which most of the other manufacturers were installing in their vehicles, Tesla chose to use battery technology from the mobile phone and camera industry – the lithium-ion battery – more than 1,500 of them in each car. This approach meant that the weight was significantly reduced, the batteries which are in small groups could be changed if there was a problem, and the cost was less than the competition. This approach, of defining the end state and then working back, produced a car that achieved the 0-60 time and had prospective customers queuing up to buy it. The problem for the company then was how to meet the demand!

From these two examples it can be seen that having a clear vision of a desired end-state or outcome can drive very different behaviours.

Rather than trying to modify what is already there, this approach focuses on creating something new.

In practice

- When you have an idea or solution in a particular area, rather than improve on what is already there, look at how things could be different. If it is an idea for a new home product, look at what 'task' the idea is trying to address and think about redefining the activity rather than improving the way a task is performed. If it is an idea for streamlining a business process or activity, seek to understand what the process does and what the current outcome is. It is worth focusing on changing the outcome rather than refining the process.

83 RECYCLE OLD IDEAS

"Learn from yesterday, live for today, hope for tomorrow. The important thing is not to stop questioning."

Albert Einstein

The idea

Our brains are wired to look for problems, solve them and move on to the next thing. Unfortunately, this behaviour means that we tend to forget what has gone before.

Revisiting our past, building on our experiences, and learning from our mistakes gives us the wherewithal to live the lives that we do. We store experiences, file them away for future reference.

Unfortunately, this often doesn't seem to happen with our ideas. We seem to consign them to the trash can of our minds as we reinvent things and solve today's problems. Although this approach allows us to function on a day-to-day basis, we lose so much by dismissing yesterday's ideas and experiences.

By keeping a record of our ideas, we can reflect and build on them as we are faced with new situations. The environment we find ourselves in and the conditions that evolve can make some elements of these ideas appropriate.

In practice

* It is vital to record your ideas and go back and revisit them from time to time. There may be some environmental conditions that make the idea unworkable but things change quickly and the idea may come of age.

  * I recommend creating an Excel spreadsheet to capture your ideas. If you have the time, try to categorise your ideas so that you can sort through them quickly when required.

  * Once a month, schedule a little time to revisit your ideas database – has anything changed that would make one of these ideas viable?

  * Could a few ideas be combined to create something new? Is there a trend in your ideas? Can you cluster them to focus on a new area for your innovation?

84 FOCUS ON THE CUSTOMER

"The key to optimising organisational performance in the short-term and succeeding in the long-term is through innovation. Innovation is the only way to effectively close the gap between customer demands and decreasing resources. Innovation allows us to do more with less."

Andrew Papageorge

The idea

Think about the customer who gets service or products from you. Make sure you understand your customer's needs and try to view the situation from their viewpoint, through their eyes, and don't rely on your own view of the world.

Putting yourself in the shoes of your customer/client/beneficiary can provide unique insights and help you formulate your ideas and thoughts. It can be hard at first as our preconceptions and experiences keep us focused on ourselves. However, through perseverance and research you can start to think like your customer and understand the world they live in!

So many times the focus is placed on the supplier or provider – looking to make it easy for them rather than thinking about the customer. Although this will benefit the supplier or provider, it can have disastrous consequences for the customer. A great example is the postal sector where much of 'innovation' focuses on the operation of the company although it is dressed up as a customer 'benefit'. Services such as letter and parcel tracking are an operational necessity and if the parcel/letter is delivered on time it is of little or no value to the customer; and even if it isn't delivered on time, the customer can see where it is but do nothing about it!

In practice

- Get to know who will be using or benefiting from your idea or solution. Find out as much as you can about them, not only the lives they live today but also the experiences they have had in the past, particularly when it has relevance to the idea or solution you have.

  - Try to see the world through their eyes; if it's a process that you are innovating around, work through the process in as much detail as you can.

- Understand the emotional side as well as the logical side of your idea. Ask yourself how it would make your customer feel. What would their experience be?

SEEK SOLITUDE

"A creation of importance can only be produced when its author isolates himself, it is a child of solitude."

Johann Wolfgang von Goethe

The idea

"Fools rush in where angels fear to tread" is an appropriate anthem for innovation. Often we get excited by the thrill of the moment and rush off to make something happen. The human mind is amazing, it can process information in the background and some of your best thinking happens when you are distracted, particularly if you are doing something physical or creative with your hands. Solitude is required for the subconscious to process and unravel problems.

Many of our leaders, including Margaret Thatcher and Mahatma Gandhi, used solitude to do their best thinking. Research has shown that in brainstorming, individuals produce more and better ideas than groups do. Studies also suggest that the path to excellence in many fields is a balance between solitude and socialising. Many creative people – artists, writers, as well as business leaders – give themselves time to think.

Don't rush into things and although there will be a creative stream of consciousness when you first have your idea or are presented with a problem, your best ideas will come sometime afterwards. In a typical brainstorming session which lasts an hour, the best ideas come in the last 20 minutes.

"The monotony and solitude of a quiet life stimulates the creative mind."

Albert Einstein

Unfortunately time is one commodity which we seem to be running short of; our 'always-on,' 'fast-food' lifestyle means that we are always on the go. The pace of life seems to be accelerating and therefore the need to stop every now and then and pause is greater. Taking stock of your life has become vital.

In practice

Set aside 30 minutes in your day to be by yourself – it could be commuting in your car, taking a bath or working in the garden. Try to switch off the pressures of the day, daydream if you like.

- Before you begin your 'solitude session', write down your idea, problem or potential solution on a card and read it to yourself. This will place it in your subconscious, allowing your brain to process thoughts in the background.

- At the end of your 30-minute session, take a few moments to reflect on the thoughts you have had; on the reverse of the card jot down any new thoughts or insights you may have had.

Visit a spa and book an hour's massage. This will give you time to clear your mind and focus on the issue at hand.

86 BENCHMARK YOUR INNOVATION

"It is impossible for employees to be innovative when they either don't know what they are expected to achieve, or are constrained by prescriptive measures."

Stephen Shapiro

The idea

Many companies today are undertaking innovation and it is important to understand how your activities are measuring up against others. In my over 15 years in innovation, the question of benchmarking is one I have had to address at least five times a year. One of the problems is that there are no international standards for innovation. As everybody's definition of innovation is slightly different, the ability to compare and benchmark is difficult to say the least.

One approach, and one which many companies take, is to measure innovation activity, that is how much innovation is taking place. This typically focuses on the number of ideas generated, the number of projects initiated, or the investment made in innovative activities. The problem with this approach is that I believe it is measuring the wrong things, and the old management maxim is that 'you get what you measure' becomes a truism. This therefore leads to much activity, which is what is being measured; but there is a possibility of little of real value being generated.

Going back to the definition of innovation, it is not just about having great ideas but more about creating value from those ideas; having a positive and beneficial outcome. This is a more difficult area to measure and it can be more subjective. However, that doesn't mean that it should not be measured. There are a number of innovation 'index' projects around the world that are aiming to fulfill the objective of measuring and benchmarking innovation outcomes, for the individual, the company and the country.

NESTA in the UK has an active Innovation Index project which aims to provide a company level benchmarking capability. The Global Innovation Index run by the Boston Consulting Group in the US is an innovation index that aims to provide a benchmark metric for countries around the world. There are many more and I suggest you do a quick search on Google for innovation index or innovation metric and this will bring up many initiatives in the area of innovation measurement.

Although there are many possible benchmark initiatives, it is important that you choose the right one for you, remembering what you are trying to achieve. Don't measure things that you don't need to, as it will distract from the real value you can derive from your initiative.

Because of the lack of an internationally agreed benchmarking standard, you may have to devise your own metrics and offer to benchmark with other companies or individuals. Although this approach means that you will be restricted to your contacts, it will provide you with a benchmark that is tailored to your specific needs. This can be a simple 20-question survey, which you circulate internally and with your benchmark partners, or a series of face-to-face interviews. The challenge of course is to ask the right questions!

In practice

Define what good innovation would look like for you; what would be an exceptional outcome of your activities?

Once you have decided what it would be, define five to ten criteria of excellence if you were to achieve this outcome. Don't restrict it to hard measures but also look at the softer, more emotional areas. A few examples are given below:

- Attitude of those working on the initiative

- The change in customers' behaviour

- Progress against target – think about real deliverables here and not just words

- Shareholder/stakeholder response to the initiative which could be financial or just support for the initiative.

- Bottom-line impact of the initiative such as monetary, PPR value or market impact.

87 LOOK FOR WHAT PEOPLE AREN'T DOING

"Observe what is with undivided awareness."

Bruce Lee

The idea

It is easy when looking to innovate in a particular area to focus on improving what is already there. True innovation, however, comes when a completely different angle is taken. Rather than following other people's trail, the real value comes when you create your own.

An example of this is the introduction of the Dyson Vacuum Cleaner in the early 1990s when the traditional market for domestic vacuum cleaners was dominated by a few multinational customers who had taken a very incremental approach to product development.

Historically, the vacuum cleaner had not changed much since its invention in 1901, when it used an air pump to create a partial vacuum to suck up dust and dirt. Most of the available vacuums relied on a disposable filter bag that collected the dust and filtered the air as it passed through the vacuum.

James Dyson visited a sawmill one day and noticed that the sawdust was removed from the air by giant industrial cyclones; he wondered if a similar principle could be used for domestic vacuum machines. After producing 5.127 prototype designs he finally produced a workable unit without a disposable bag, which he tried to license to the current market leaders. No one was interested, probably because the disposable bag market was worth in excess of $500 million; so this new idea was a threat to this profitable market.

Dyson decided to go it alone and set up his first factory in 1993, and the DC01 became the biggest selling vacuum cleaner in the UK in just 18 months.

In this example James Dyson looked at the market for vacuum cleaners in a completely different way; he chose to look at what people were not doing rather than what they were doing. By adopting this approach he changed the whole market for cleaners, not only in the UK but globally. The historic incumbent manufacturers are now finding that they are forced to license Dyson's approach to maintain a share in the market, and the disposable bag market has shrunk by 60%.

In practice

- In the area you are interested in innovating, write down all the existing players and try to think about their strengths and weaknesses, and try to understand their strategy.

- Once you have the list of players and their attributes, try the following:

  - Try reversing the strategy or strengths – if they play to a particular market think about other markets.

  - Look at their weaknesses and see if there is an opportunity to turn these into your strengths.

  - Think about the market for your idea/solution as a whole and try to define the pressures and drivers for this market.

  - Consider who isn't a player in this market – how would somebody like Google, Apple or Virgin enter the market or solve the problem?

88 HARVEST IDEAS FROM UNUSUAL SOURCES

"Simple solutions seldom are. It takes a very unusual mind to undertake analysis of the obvious."

Alfred North Whitehead

The idea

Don't just rely on your usual sources of ideas. Look for ideas in unusual places. One of the traits of a great innovator is constant curiosity and great observation. When you are out shopping or at the gym, keep an eye out for ideas that could help. Brilliant ideas can come from the most unexpected places.

One example of this is a story from a lingerie company in the UK which was finding it difficult to sell brassieres (bras) as women were reluctant to buy them online since they couldn't try them on. The ones that did try to buy online tended to order a few, try them on and then return the ones that didn't fit. This caused problems for the supplier as, due to the potential hygiene problems, they couldn't sell the returned items. They tried a few ideas, including asking people to try them on with a plastic bag as a barrier but they couldn't guarantee that the customer adhered to the guidelines.

Every bra manufacturer uses a different 'form' for their garments and therefore the shape of each manufacturer's goods is slightly different. This factor is incredibly important for the customer, as they need to find the one that fits them best, and is the most comfortable.

When out shopping one day in a supermarket with his wife, the CEO saw some avocados packaged in plastic blister packs in the vegetable section. His thoughts went to his problem and the next day he ordered some plastic 'blisters' in the shape of each manufacturer's bras, in a range of sizes. He sent these out to a few of the customers so they could try on the shapes, and the result was amazing. Suddenly customers could find the best shape and most comfortable fit before ordering – the result was that his sales trebled in six months.

This story shows how a random event such as food shopping can trigger a thought, an idea/link that can cause true innovation. It would have been easy for this CEO to have just got on with the shopping; however, linking blister packs to lingerie created a noteworthy idea which cost a few pence to implement but had a massive benefit.

The secret is to remain curious and constantly look for possible linkages with your idea or solution. I would even suggest that every time you go out – whether on a business trip, a shopping trip or a vacation – take a notepad with you to jot down any ideas or insights you gain from your surroundings.

In practice

- Next time you go out write down your idea or solution in a notebook. Keep it concise and simple.

- Wherever you find yourself, look around you and force yourself to look for linkages and insights. It will be hard at first but persist for at least 10 minutes and you will find that it becomes easier towards the end of this time.

- Repeat this exercise a few times and you will find yourself constantly looking for these linkages and insights.

SUSPEND JUDGMENT

"*To the person who does not know where he wants to go there is no favourable wind.*"

Seneca

The idea

When generating ideas or solutions to a problem, try not to dismiss your thoughts too quickly but instead, make sure you have explored the idea fully and looked at it from all angles. This is particularly important when thinking about changing an existing product or service or building on it.

Rather than think about what could stop you achieving your goals, suspend judgment and think about what you could do if you had no constraints – if you had no barriers to your success.

Again, this will not come naturally at first, as we have built up preconceptions and experiences over our life. Our previous failures and successes will colour our ideas and behaviours, and will define how we think and particularly how we approach the problem or idea.

One approach to innovation is to suspend all judgment – assume anything is possible and you have no barriers to achieving whatever you want. Although this may sound a little strange, you will be quite surprised by what is possible if you just clear away all the clutter of your self-limiting beliefs.

In practice

Think about a time in your life when you had a great idea or were trying to achieve something and you didn't manage to achieve it – not because you couldn't but because you believed you couldn't. What stopped you? How did your thinking alter your beliefs about the way you approach things?

Try the 'if you absolutely could not fail' exercise. Think about your idea or solution and then look at what the outcome would be 'if you absolutely could not fail' – this will be your goal for your plan.

- If this was the outcome what would you have to do to achieve it – who would you need to help you and what resources would you need?

- At this stage, don't think about the barriers and negatives – just focus on the positives.

- After you have exhausted your list of positives, turn to the potential barriers.

For each barrier you come up with, write down five ways to overcome it.

- You may just find that what you thought was a barrier is not that at all, and achieving your goal is easier than you expected.

STIMULATE INNOVATION AND INSIGHT

"In the world of words, the imagination is one of the forces of nature."

Wallace Stevens

The idea

Introducing randomness into the equation is a traditional way of getting stimulation for new ideas or solutions. Take a dictionary or any book, open a page and find a noun. Look for associations with your idea and list them down. Look for links in the words and ask yourself if this gives you any new insights.

This technique can be used with pictures, fictional and non-fictional characters, films, television shows or any other element that will introduce a degree of randomness to your thinking.

To obtain your random element, open any magazine or newspaper and pick an article or photo at random. Next think about your idea or solution and look for associations or linkages between your thoughts and the picture/text. Try not to be too prescriptive in your thinking and expand your idea/solution as far as you can go.

The photo on the right is one I took in Cornwall whilst on vacation. To use this as stimulation for our idea for dog repellent trousers for a post person, let's look at the elements of the photo – there is a bright blue sky, the houses seem to be a jumble, there are a number of boats anchored in the bay and there are strong reflections.

The photo is roughly split into thirds with the top where all the real interest is. If we translate this into our idea for dog repellent trousers we can associate the proportions of the trousers with the photo, i.e. only the bottom two-thirds need to be protected. Maybe the trousers need to be reflective and have a 'jumble' of pockets to keep things in. The trousers could be 'anchored' to the post person's jacket to protect against the weather. You can see from this example that even a seemingly obscure picture can have associations and linkages to your idea.

In practice

Gather a wide range of magazines and newspapers and open three or four at random and pick an article or a photo from each.

- If you have bought them, I suggest you cut them out and stick each on a separate piece of paper.

- Write your idea/solution on the top of the paper and then list any association or linkage you can think of for each one.

When you have your linkages/associations written down, go through them and see if there is any commonality or groups of ideas.

Has this given you any new insights?

91 TRY WRITING DIFFERENTLY

"Writing something down when you're thinking about it, even if you don't review what you've written again, is a way of giving weight to the thought process."

John Briggs

The idea

Instead of relying on pure inspiration, set your topic or theme for your idea or solution and start writing about it; don't worry about making sense at this stage. Getting down your thoughts, your aspirations and your ideas on paper will help to rationalise them and may even bring new insights, which you can build on.

If you are used to writing business reports, try writing about the topic area as poetry, a children's story, a murder mystery or even science fiction. Who would the characters be? What scenario would you put them in, what environment would you base your story in? Writing in a different style will make you think about things differently and of course it will play to a different audience.

You probably won't produce any great works of fiction with this exercise but you will be able to think about how to convey your idea or solution in a new way. If you include characters in the story, these may be ones you want to help you achieve your goals. Maybe they face adversaries and problems, which you see as barriers to your success; write down how they overcame them.

There are many structures for stories if you try searching the Internet. The one I like and have used many times is the Heroes' journey also referred to as a monomyth. This structure can be seen in *Harry Potter, Star Wars,* even the *Magnificent Seven* and many other films and was first introduced in 1949 by Joseph Campbell in *The Hero With A Thousand Faces.* The original 'journey' had 17 steps but this can be reduced to simplify things for the purpose of writing your innovation story.

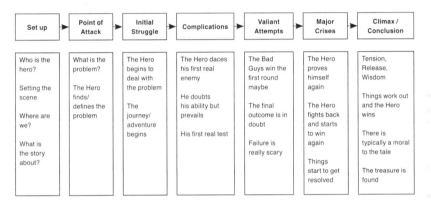

Figure 32: Heroes' Journey

In practice

Try writing your idea/solution using the Heroes' journey format and see what comes out – the worksheet included in this section may help you formulate your ideas.

MORPHOLOGICAL MODELLING

"The successful person is always seeking out the next area for growth, mapping out the next plan, working on the next idea, pursuing the next opportunity, looking for the next challenge, aiming at the next target."

Dennis Waitley

The idea

This technique is an extension of one first developed in the 1940s by Fritz Zwicky who was a Swiss astrophysicist based at the California Institute of Technology. The technique is based on the relationship between attributes and characteristics of a particular problem or need.

Although based on Zwicky's initial work, it has been further developed to encompass problem solving and innovation.

To use the technique, the first step is to identify the problem or need and gain an agreement on the definition. Once you have a clear definition, the next step is to list all the possible solutions or ideas; 5 – 7 potential solutions/ideas is a good number to keep things manageable. Once you have your possible solutions the next step is to list all the issues, risks, benefits, capabilities that would be required to create a great outcome. Listing these on separate post-it notes is a way of capturing these as they can be used to group/sort in the next step.

Hopefully there will be some duplication in these and consolidation can take place. The next stage is to group the post-it notes into easily understood groups – again five to seven groups is manageable. Interestingly seven possible solutions with seven 'values' still adds up to nearly a million possible permutations!

Once you have your 7 by 7 matrix, the task of analysing the information can take place. I find it is good at this point to stand back and see if anything obvious stands out before I get into too much detail. Sometimes there will be a solution that stands out above the others or a group of values that you didn't expect. In the Figure below I have created an example based on declining mail volumes.

Once the matrix has been created, it can be cut up to create long strips with the values/ideas below. Once the lists are prepared the next step is to move the strips up and down to create new combinations of ideas, values etc. This should provide some new insights. The following table shows this analysis.

Problem: Volume of mail is declining

Educate children to write letters	Link mail to social media	Make collecting stamps 'cool'	Pay people to send mail	Emphasise the security aspects of mail
Letter writing competition	Facebook postcard service	Put celebrity faces on stamps	Launch a Post points service	Offer guaranteed secure mail service
Sponsor a penpal campaign	LinkedIn job application app	Get teenagers to design stamps	Build a database of all customers and businesses	People don't trust the postman
Teachers don't know how to write letters	Teenagers don't write letters	Only dead people can have their faces on stamps	Set up a competition – who sends the most mail wins	Delivery of mail not guaranteed
Paper is expensive	Discount rates for sending to Facebook friends	Technology stamps	Get advertisers to sponsor social mail	Advertise the lack of security of email
Set up children's writing groups	Bring physical mail into social media applications	QR code stamps	TV show based on mail	Develop secure envelope which cannot be opened without token

Figure 33: Example of Morphological Modelling Matrix

In practice

- Clearly define your idea or solution and write it down.

- Brainstorm a list of possible solutions/ideas.

- For each potential solution write down a list of ideas, values, issues etc.

- Look for commonality and group the ideas, values, issues, etc. Try and rationalise down to five to seven for each solution/idea.

- Undertake the analysis as described in the main section of the chapter.

- Write down any new ideas you have come out with.

93 ASK CHALLENGING QUESTIONS

"Rowing harder doesn't help if the boat is headed in the wrong direction."

Kenichi Ohmae

The idea

Asking the basic 'what if' questions is a fun way to develop more creative thoughts. Ask those crazy questions, and then find a way to make them not so crazy. Then try to refine a few of them into something practical and usable.

A good place to start is the Who, What, Why, Where, When and How questions. Once you have framed your idea or solution apply these six questions to it.

- Who is going to benefit?

- What will be changed by your idea/solution?

- Why is your idea or solution different from what already exists?

- Where will the most value be derived?

- When will your goal be reached, be realistic!

- How will you go about achieving your goal?

These may not seem to be very challenging questions but they will at least get you started. The next step is to write down the assumptions you have made for each of your answers. Are these assumptions realistic? Could they be defended if challenged? What other assumptions could you have used?

Challenge each of your answers to the original six questions. What if you reversed the answers? Would this change your approach?

"If I had an hour to solve a problem and my life depended on the solution, I would spend the first 55 minutes determining the proper question to ask, for once I know the proper question, I could solve the problem in less than five minutes."

Albert Einstein

There are, I am sure, many other questions you could ask and as Albert Einstein states, time should be taken getting to the right question – once you have this then the answers should be relatively easy. Here are some thoughts about getting to the right questions:

1. Are the questions relevant to the real life and the situation or environment you are focusing on?

2. Is this a genuine question to which I/we really don't know the answer?

3. What 'task' do I want these questions to do? When asking these questions what response do I want; a new insight, a challenge to an existing preconception, the meaning of something or an understanding?

4. Is this question likely to provoke new thinking? Will it just give people the opportunity to focus on past problems and obstacles?

5. What assumptions or beliefs are embedded in the way these questions are constructed?

6. Is this question likely to move your thoughts forward or just reinforce your current thinking?

In practice

- Try answering the following 10 questions about your idea/ solution:

  - What question, if answered, could make the most difference to the future of the idea?

  - What's important to you about your idea/solution and why do you care?

  - What's the deeper purpose (the big 'why') that is really worthy of your best effort? Why should people be interested in your idea?

  - What opportunities can you see in your idea or solution?

  - What do you know so far? Are there still things you need to learn about your idea?

  - What are the dilemmas you still face and how can you resolve them?

  - What assumptions do you need to test or challenge in thinking about your idea?

  - What is missing from your thinking? What else do you need to know before you can progress?

  - What's been your/our major learning, insight, or discovery so far?

  - What would someone who had a very different perspective and set of beliefs/values, think about your idea?

94 ACTIVELY SEEK OUT THE OPPOSITE

"No great man ever complains of lack of opportunity."

Ralph Waldo Emerson

The idea

Look at one of your beliefs or opinions and ask, what if the opposite were true? This technique can be used for many areas when thinking about your idea.

- Beliefs – What if all your beliefs were reversed – you believed the opposite of what you do? How would this change your thinking? What different perspective would this give you? By reversing your beliefs you provide yourself with a completely different view of the world.

- Experiences – What if your experiences were reversed? Suppose what had worked for you in the past had been a failure, and what had been a failure in the past was an amazing success? Would this change the way you approached your idea or solution?

- Assumptions – Think about the assumptions you have made and then try to reverse them; change them round and think about what the opposite would be. Be as expansive as you can be when thinking about this. Don't be confined by your beliefs.

- Value – What would be different if you had opposite values to those you currently hold? Would this change your idea or your solution? Would it make you do things differently or involve different people?

- People – What if you had people working with you who were the opposite of you? How would this change your situation? Would you do things differently? Would it provide new insights?

By applying opposites to these areas, you will challenge your ideas and the approach you are taking. This will provide you with new insights and potentially allow you to build on your ideas and thoughts.

In practice

It is worth documenting these ideas and revisiting them on a regular basis to challenge your current state of thinking. As with many of the techniques in this book, it is worth coming back to them on a regular basis to make sure you are still on track with your thinking.

95 DITCH GROUP BRAINSTORMING

The idea

Ditch group brainstorming because it often causes people to simply follow the most dominant member of the group. I have found on so many occasions that when working with larger groups brainstorming new ideas, there are a few people who dominate the session and the rest sit back and watch. This gives the passive members the opportunity to opt out of the idea generation process and thereby opt out of any decisions that are made.

Studies have shown that individuals working alone can generate more and better ideas than when working as a group. A better approach, I have found, is to either generate ideas yourself or have people come up with ideas on their own, and then meet to discuss them. This works well with geographically dispersed teams, and particularly where you are hoping to generate ideas from customers.

When generating ideas you can use post-it notes as you would in a group brainstorming session or mind-mapping software, which is freely available on the Internet. The secret is to have a 'friction-free' environment which allows you to generate and document as many ideas as possible. As with working with a group, categorise your ideas and then group them. At this stage, it is worth getting input from a wider group as you may be constraining your thinking through your beliefs.

There are, however, many benefits of group brainstorming in that everyone in the group gains a better understanding of the problem, and there is a feeling of common ownership of outcome of the session.

In practice

- Set aside some time to brainstorm ideas around your topic area – give yourself at least an hour. Make sure you have no distractions and you have plenty of paper and pens.

- Categorise your ideas and then group them into appropriate areas.

- Ask for input from a wider group – friends, family or maybe even prospective customers.

96 THINK OF THE GOOD AND THE BAD

"Every act of creation is first of all an act of destruction."

Picasso

The idea

If you're thinking only of the good ideas, you're not really being creative, since you have decided which is good or bad based on your existing preconceptions and beliefs.

The idea of 'good' and 'bad' is subjective based on your current thoughts and experiences. You can take advantage of these concepts and build on your ideas using your bad ideas to challenge your thinking and maybe bring you new insights.

The secret of getting the best out of bad ideas is to look for the good in them. Think in which context the bad idea would be good.

For each bad idea that you come up with, write down five good things about it.

A bad idea might be a car with no engine; the good thing about this would be that it would be environmentally friendly, would be cheap to run, light and potentially cheap to produce and lastly, would not need to stop to refuel. Of course, this concept would never be viable as it would have no motive power but if you took the concept further, maybe the power would come from the road surface or from some other external source. As you can see from this approach, what started out as a bad idea can be turned around to provide some useful insights into vehicles of the future.

In practice

- List all the bad points about your idea or solution.

- For each bad thing list five good things, then group them together. Are there any trends or insights that you can draw from this exercise?

TRIM THE FAT

The idea

When Michelangelo was asked how he made the David, he said it was simple – that he merely took away "everything that wasn't". The same holds for you – keep it simple – take away anything that isn't essential to delivering your idea or solution.

A great example is the Apple iPod. If you look at the interfaces being developed at the time of the iPod launch, you will find that they were complicated with buttons for everything. The iPod, on the other hand, introduced a simple wheel interface that allowed the user to access everything through a single interface. By taking away all the clutter, Apple revolutionised the way we listen to music, and, what is more important, the company redefined what was acceptable to users.

Start by simplifying the process or topic you are interested in. Take away all the non-essentials to achieving the goal – all the things that distract from the process or idea. Once you have the essentials, you can look at how you can innovate around the core process or idea.

This technique works well for complex business processes that have evolved over time. In large organisations, very few people challenge the status quo and often add new steps to an existing process to solve local problems. These additional steps can add significant cost and time to a process as well as complicating it for users and customers. By trimming away all the fripperies you get down to the essential elements, the essential steps of the process. Take care not to get bogged down in the process itself and focus on the outcome instead.

Once you have your idea or solution stripped down to the essentials, it is time to look at how you can deliver it. Again look at the minimum required to make it happen; rather than have a Rolls Royce solution think about the Model T version.

Creating this 'fat free' version of your idea or solution will help when it comes to costing materials and resources, particularly people. Having the essence of the idea or solution will provide you with a unique view of what you are trying to achieve, and how you can achieve it.

In practice

- Take your idea or solution and strip it down to the essentials. If it is a process, focus on the outcome it is trying to achieve and look at the basic steps you would require to achieve it. If it is an idea for a new product or service, think about the minimal that would be required to achieve success.

- Once you have the minimal version, it is easy to add things later for greater value.

98 TOLERATE AMBIGUITY

"You will discover very little creativity in yourself without the discomfort of confusion, uncertainty, anxiety and ambiguity."

Jeff Mauzy and Richard Harriman

The idea

We all like certainty in our lives, it gives us a sense of comfort and a certain security in our daily activities. However, when dealing with innovation and creativity, certainty is a luxury we probably cannot afford. Innovative ideas tend to come in bits and pieces and develop over time, creating uncertainty which tends to be very uncomfortable. Without time and the ability to tolerate ambiguity, you may jump to a less than optimal or simply wrong solution.

An idea often does not come to mind in a flash, but rather evolves over time – sometimes over many years. This is important as it gives the brain time to think through all the angles, how to overcome the obstacles and get to the heart of the matter – the real nub of the idea or concept.

When thinking through your idea or solution, you will find that there are many things that you do not and maybe cannot know at any one time. There may also be many options for your idea or solution, and often these will not be completed until very late in the innovation process. It is important that you do not try to 'batten down' these options too soon in the process.

Although it is natural to reduce the ambiguity as far as possible, it may affect your idea or solution. My mantra when thinking about a new idea or concept is to "keep as loose as you can as long as you can." It is interesting that children tolerate ambiguity better than adults do – we seem to become less tolerant the older we get.

This approach can be uncomfortable for many people, and it may be hard to tolerate this level of ambiguity for any length of time. Try to force yourself to keep your options open for as long as you can – you will benefit from it in the long run!

The ability to tolerate ambiguity also seems to be linked to the ability to tolerate and embrace risk. True innovators feel the need to embrace and challenge risk, to fight against the status quo and embrace uncertainty.

Note: Another area of ambiguity which you might come across is in the way you describe things. This may be an area where ambiguity might not be tolerated quite so well!

In practice

- Think about all the ambiguities you have in your idea/solution. How many of them do you have to nail down now and how many can you leave open?

- Write down your idea in less than 29 words and ask a friend or family member to read it and then describe what they think it is. Did they get it right? If not re-write it and try again.

FIND THE SPACES

The idea

Look for areas where things aren't happening. We tend to concentrate on areas where there is activity, where there is interest. Some of the biggest innovations happen where people are not looking.

This is a complex and often difficult aspect to address, but it can be most fruitful in the long run. By focusing on things that others are not doing you might be able to make a real difference.

I use a simple approach to find new areas to become interested in; for one week I read all the business magazines, websites and newspapers I can find to get a 'feeling' for current trends and the focus of company activities. I tend to focus on an industry or sector I am interested in purely to cut down on the 'noise' and get a better sense of what is happening. If everyone in the utility sector is talking about customer service it is probably not worth trying to innovate in this area but instead look at pricing or service delivery as an area for innovation.

In practice

- Spend time researching the area you are interested in – through magazines, newspapers and the Internet.

- Spend at least 30 minutes per day for a couple of weeks getting a sense of what is happening in this sector. At the end of each day, write down any insights you may have had about what isn't being talked about, or what is not there that you would have expected to see.

- Write down a list of the 'white spaces' you have found at the end of the two weeks; these will be the areas for you to focus on.

KEEP ON TRYING

"The only source of profit, the only reason to invest in companies in the future, is their ability to innovate and their ability to differentiate."

Jeffrey Immelt

The idea

If one thing isn't working, don't keep trying until you give up. Try a new approach, a different angle; think about the situation from someone else's viewpoint, ask a child for an idea.

It is easy to give up if you find things are not working well, or if you have met with an obstacle to achieving your goal. Being an innovator you will probably want to move on to something else, find new stimulation, an outlet for your creative juices. You should guard against this as it could mean giving up on what might be your best idea.

The secret is to try a new approach, find new stimulation, talk to different people or find a new angle on your existing idea. Since it is likely that you are not going to do this by yourself, find help from other sources.

It is important that you keep your vision for your idea or solution clear in your mind as this will give you a purpose for your activities.

Be willing to try new things and move into areas others find impossible; this is where innovation will happen.

In practice

- Think about five different approaches you could take to bringing your idea/solution to fruition. Don't be restricted to approaches that you have tried out before; be open to try out new things. Do this early on in your thinking so that if you come up against an obstacle you will have other ways to approach it.

APPENDIX

Weekly innovation activity list

To change your attitude and your behaviour, it is a good idea to employ a range of techniques on a regular basis. To prompt you I have put together a list of 52 techniques which you can try, one for each week of the year. The list is in alphabetical order but you can rearrange it if you prefer:

- Advertise your needs, get other people on board to contribute to your idea.

- Apply constraints to your thinking, don't forget scarce resources breed innovation.

- Ask yourself "How would this work upside down, or what if it was reversed?"

- Avoid analysis to paralysis – keep things as simple as you can.

- Be thoughtful of others and the world around you. Take time to understand other people's work area, problems and issues.

- Be true to yourself, develop a unique personal style.

- Break your routines, do things differently.

- Celebrate small successes, take time to thank people for their work, particularly if it involves innovative activity.

- Challenge conventional thinking and wisdom.

- Change your perspective on life, find new environments, engage with new friends, start new hobbies, adopt new thinking.

- Do a random act of kindness, try being kind to the people you meet on your daily activities.

- Do odd things that you wouldn't normally do.

- Don't be afraid to ask – find your inner child.

- Don't do what everyone else is doing but instead, find new ways to challenge yourself.

- Don't be afraid of strange ideas and thoughts; look at things differently, try reversing things, change positives to negatives.

- Don't celebrate too soon.

- Embrace and pursue uncertainty.

- Embrace irritations, find ways of engaging with those people around you who have a habit of irritating you.

- Embrace simplicity.

- Embrace technology, take time to learn a new application or a new technology.

- Encourage yourself to be inquisitive and curious, ask lots of questions.

- Find odd people to hang out with.

- Find ways to relax, give yourself time to think.

- Find your eccentric self.

- Find out about things that you wouldn't normally be interested in; read magazines, attend meetings, talk to people.

- Force randomness into your life; use random objects, words, images, websites, magazines etc., to stimulate thought.

- Get off the beaten track. Explore and bounce off new experiences and people.

- Give yourself stretch goals and targets.

- Go for the radical – don't put up with the incremental.

- Have a healthy disregard for conventions, be skeptical.

- Have conversations with people, not discussions, and listen twice as much as you speak.

- Introduce people to each other, you might be surprised at what spins off from their conversations.

- Keep others off-balance and spread confusion around you.

- Laugh out loud, find humour in things.

- Make the impossible possible, find an idea or a solution which has stalled and use your influence, knowledge and skills to make it happen.

- Make your ideas public – encourage discussion and debate about your ideas.

- Don't justify or rationalise your ideas and have an open mind. Take time to re-think your idea without any constraints.

- People often haven't got a clue about what they want – don't forget that people don't know what they don't know. If you didn't have to consider a customer, what would you do?

- Poke people in the eye, challenge their views, beliefs, routines and processes.

- Pursue your passions, do something that you have always wanted to do but have never had time for.

- Read, read, read. Read blogs, books, periodicals, magazines; not just ones you would normally read but also those you wouldn't think of reading.

- Set up a blog and promote your activity or interests.

- Study and apply innovations and technology from sectors that are completely different from the one you operate in.

- Take a break from technology. Try and minimise your use of technology for a week.

- Take courses that you wouldn't normally take – photography, jewellery making, watercolour painting – to give you new perspectives.

- Take on uncomfortable and difficult projects.

- Take a vacation to an interesting and stimulating place so that you can see the world through other people's eyes.

- Throw away the rule book. Don't play by other people's rules but invent your own.

- Tinker, experiment, practice trial and error. Adopt the Google 20% 'own time' to give yourself time to try new things.

- Understand how you can re-invent yourself – your style, your clothing, your behaviour.

- Value other people's thoughts – learn to actively listen.

- Vary your working and thinking environment.

FURTHER READING

Books

- *A Kick in the Seat of the Pants*, Roger von Oech
- *A Whack on the Side of the Head*, Roger von Oech
- *Whack Pack*, Roger von Oech
- *Black Swan*, Nassim Nicholas Talebe
- *Lateral Thinking*, Edward De Bono
- *Six Thinking Hats*, Edward De Bono
- *Teach Your Child How to Think*, Edward De Bono
- *Use Both Sides of Your Brain*, Tony Buzan
- *Tribes*, Seth Godin
- *Why Men Don't Listen and Women Can't Read Maps*, Barbara Pease and Alan Pease
- *How Doctors Think*, Jerome E. Groopman
- *Leaders: Strategies for Taking Charge*, Bennis, W., Nanus, B. (2007)
- *Thriving on Chaos: Handbook for a Management Revolution*, Tom Peters (2007)
- *Understanding Comics*, Scott McCloud
- *Humans in Universe*, Richard Buckminster Fuller, Anwar S. Dil (1983)
- *101 Unuseless Japanese Inventions: The Art of Chindogu*, Kawakami and Papia (1995)

99 More Unuseless Japanese Inventions, Kawakami and Papia (1997)

"Developmental sequence in small groups". *Psychological Bulletin*, Bruce Tuckman (1995)

If Life is a Game, These Are the Rules, Cherie Carter-Scott, Ph.D (1998)

Gerald Ratner: The Rise and Fall... and Rise Again, Gerald Ratner (2007)

Websites

TED: www.ted.com

Creativity Techniques: http://www.mycoted.com/ Category:Creativity_Techniques

Creativity Techniques: http://www.mindtools.com/

Macro photographs: http://albertlleal.com/

Blogging sites

Blogger: www.blogger.com

Typepad: www.typepad.com

Survey Sites

SurveyMonkey: www.surveymonkey.com

Search engines

Google: www.google.com

Dogpile: www.dogpile.com

ABOUT THE AUTHOR

Howard is a thought leader in the field of innovation, having actively worked in the area for the last 15 years. He has held a number of senior roles in corporate innovation in both the UK and the US, and held consultancy roles in the UK, leading an innovation network of over 40 FTSE 100 companies. He is currently running his own innovation and foresight consultancy.

A published author on innovation (*Ten Steps to Innovation Heaven*), Howard is also a frequent international conference speaker and Internet blogger. He is passionate about innovation and technology, particularly their integration in, and impact on, society and business. He initially trained as a photographer before moving on to become an engineer, and finally placed his career firmly in the path of strategy and innovation in the corporate arena.

He has a diverse range of hobbies that includes stained glass, motorcycling and travel. His most recent project is building his own Caterham kit car.

100 Great Presentation Ideas
From leading companies around the world
Patrick Forsyth

Do you get nervous about making presentations? How much preparation do you do for a presentation? What are the secrets to making an impactful presentation?

Presentations matter. There can be a great deal hanging on them and rarely, if one fails to work, do you get a second chance. A poor presentation can blight a plan, a proposal, a reputation... even a career. But making a good one is not easy, as a quotation from Sir George Jessel makes clear: The human brain is a wonderful thing. It starts working the moment you are born and never stops until you stand up to speak in public. If you identify with this all too readily, your fears and experience will only be made worse if you make a presentation without understanding what makes it work, without adequate preparation or founded only on some irrational belief that you can wing it.

Presentation success can be ensured, however, if you adopt an active approach, understand the way it works, and deploy the right techniques. The 100 approaches and ideas contained in this book have been proven and can be used or adapted to underpin and enliven your presentation and maximize its effectiveness. Some are self contained, affecting a moment of what you do; others can influence your whole approach. Anyone can present in an acceptable, workmanlike way, or even excel at it, if they go about it in the right way.

ISBN 978-981-4276-91-7 / £8.99 PAPERBACK

100 Great Marketing Ideas
From leading companies around the world
Jim Blythe

Do you know how to use promotional gifts that really promote? Do you have a startling brand? Do you know how to discourage the customers you *don't* want? Or even *how* to spot them coming?

Marketing moves fast—competitors come up with new ideas to steal your business every day, so you need to stay ahead of the game. This book can help! Written in an engaging and lively manner, it gives you 100 ideas from real companies, ideas that have been tried and tested. The ideas are thought provoking and adaptable to most businesses—some are no-brainers (which, nevertheless, are under-used), while others are subtle and surprising.

Whether you are running a small business of your own, working in marketing for a big company, or advising others, this book will be an invaluable addition to your briefcase.

ISBN 978-0-462-09942-2 / £8.99 PAPERBACK

100 Great Leadership Ideas
From leading companies around the world
Jonathan Gifford

Do you have a new vision for your organization's long-term future? Are you harnessing the collective intelligence of the organization? Will you devolve decision making to a level closer to the customer? Is your organization making a contribution to the common good?

The list of attributes and behavioural skills needed by any modern leader is dauntingly long. This book uses the collective wisdom of over 130 outstanding modern leaders to select and present the most significant leadership ideas, concepts and practices that have been proven to work in today's business environment.

The ideas have allowed successful modern leaders to deliver exceptional results in a rapidly changing world. They confirm that we must move away from the old-fashioned 'command and control' model of leadership and develop a more collaborative, consensual and inspirational approach to running modern organizations.

The great leaders of the future will achieve success through empowerment and devolved decision-making processes and by creating organizational structures that successfully harness the creative energies, innovatory skills and adaptive capacity of every member of the organization. The challenge for modern leaders is, if anything, even greater than before, as some of the old comfort zones of central command are stripped away. But since leadership is all about change, leaders must themselves be prepared to embrace the new leadership challenges of the future.

ISBN 978-981-4276-90-0 / £8.99 PAPERBACK

100 Great PR Ideas

From leading companies around the world

Jim Blythe

Do you know how to turn a crisis into a triumph? Can you write a press release that gets you thousands of pounds worth of free publicity? Do you know how to hijack your competitors' PR and turn it against them?

This book can help! PR is exciting, it is essential, and it is easy to do—once you know how. Thousands of companies use PR to generate free publicity, to win over customers, to defuse criticism and potential threats from governments, and to put their name in the public eye. This book gives you 100 ideas from real companies, ideas that have worked time and time again to create the right impression.

Written in a lively, engaging style, this book gives you the ammunition you need to take the fight to the enemy. Whether you are running a small business or work for a major firm, or whether you are new to PR or have been in the business for years, this book has something for you.

ISBN 978-0-462-09949-1 / £8.99 PAPERBACK

100 Great Sales Ideas
From leading companies around the world
Patrick Forsyth

Do you "climb the stairs" to find new clients? Do you have a spoken logo? And how do you cope when you meet that prospect you just can't get along with?

Selling—the personal interaction between buyer and seller—is a key part of the overall marketing process. However much interest other marketing has generated, selling must convert that interest and turn it into action to buy. In today's market a key issue is to differentiate, to ensure your approach sets you apart from competition. A creative attitude to sales activity is even more important when faced with difficult markets or economic times.

Selling success can be made more certain if you adopt an active approach, understand the way it works, and deploy the right techniques in the right way. This book will help you achieve that success by providing a resource to assist the continuous process of analysis and review that is necessary to create sales excellence.

100 Great Sales Ideas is a book to dip into rather than read all in one sitting. The book contains 100 self-contained sales ideas from companies as varied as Raffles Hotel (Singapore), Sony and Amazon, with observations from Cathay Pacific Airways and Waterstone's bookshops, among others. As the author, Patrick Forsyth, states: "One new idea may take you a step forward in terms of results and customer satisfaction; a steady stream of them will secure your future."

ISBN 978-0-462-09961-3 / £8.99 PAPERBACK